ZULUFIGHT

- Fight To Win System -

By Instructor Zulu

ZuluFight Fight To Win System, Copyright © 2014 Zulu Tactical LLC. All rights reserved. No part of this book may be reproduced or transmitted in any form or by any means, electronic or mechanical, including but not limited to: photocopy, recording, or by any other information storage and retrieval system, without the written permission from the author Instructor Zulu and Zulu Tactical LLC.

Dedication

"Si Vis Pacem Para Bellum"

—Vegetius—

This system is dedicated to the thousands of brave men and women who have committed their lives to a cause greater than themselves. They stand guard each passing day, forming an unbreakable wall of defense which ensures the integrity of our every freedom. They continue the selfless act of service, by which legions of heroic patriots before have paid the ultimate sacrifice, to secure and defend peace no matter the cost. May we live each day with the gratitude and determination, careful to never take our peace filled privileges for granted. May we always remember the cost and may we each have the courage, fortitude and perseverance to stand in defense of the values and morals which make us 'Free'.

Table of Contents

Introduction..p. 7

Chapter 1: Fighting To Win...p. 12

Chapter 2: ZuluScience..p. 20

Chapter 3: To See or Not To See...................................p. 41

Chapter 4: Training For Mastery....................................p. 50

Instructions...p. 69

Handgun Exercises..p. 71
- C.Q.B. Ready..p. 72
- SUL Ready...p. 75
- Holstered..p. 78
- Tactical Reload...p. 83
- Combat Reload...p. 85
- Type 1 Malfunction...p. 87
- Type 2 Malfunction...p. 89
- Type 3 Malfunction...p. 91
- Decreasing Par-Time Handgun.............................p. 93
  - C.Q.B. Ready...p. 94
  - SUL Ready...p. 96
  - Holstered...p. 98
  - Seated...p. 100
  - Seated to Tactical Stance.............................p. 102
  - Tactical Reload...p. 104

- 5 -

- Combat Reload..p. 106
  - Type 1 Malfunction..p. 108
  - Type 2 Malfunction..p. 110
  - Type 3 Malfunction..p. 112

Long Gun Exercises...p. 114
- Index Ready..p. 115
- Low Index Ready..p. 118
- Sling Carry...p. 121
- Tactical Reload...p. 122
- Combat Reload..p. 126
- Type 1 Malfunction..p. 129
- Type 2 Malfunction..p. 131
- Type 3 Malfunction..p. 133
- Decreasing Par-Time Long Gun....................p. 134
  - Index Ready..p. 136
  - Low Index Ready....................................p. 138
  - Sling Carry...p. 140
  - Tactical Reload......................................p. 142
  - Combat Reload.....................................p. 144
  - Type 1 Malfunction...............................p. 146
  - Type 2 Malfunction...............................p. 148
  - Type 3 Malfunction...............................p. 150

Images...p. 153

Threat Target..p. 203

ABCs Tactical Training Aides Bio............................p. 205

ZuluShield Bio..p. 206

ZuluLinks..p. 207

Introduction

"Every battle is won before it's ever fought."
—*Sun Tzu*—

You possess a firearm, but do you possess the knowledge and skill to safely and effectively employ such a dangerous tool to actually defend your life or someone else's? Do you understand the dynamics of combat and, more importantly the 'Science' behind it? Most people don't. In fact, most law enforcement and military professionals lack this all important knowledge and skill set. The reality is that defending one's self with a firearm is no different than a police or military shootout, no different than an old west showdown at high-noon. When the bullets start flying, the realities, disadvantages, struggles, consequences and overall dynamics of a confrontation with an armed intruder in your home, is no different than a SWAT Hostage Rescue takedown. The surest way of winning a gun battle is achieved through skill and preparation.

The key to the perfect tactical solution for a deadly encounter, is completely and utterly depended upon your preparation beforehand. You must arrive to the deadly encounter already prepared and already equipped, with three all important qualities:

1. Without sound combatives training, your fancy new firearm is useless and in all reality places you and others at grater risk.

2. Without sound understanding of the laws associated with Self-Defense, there's no way for you to develop a decision making process which provides reasonable responses to perceived threats.

3. Without a sound Legal Defense plan, should you be forced to actually use Deadly Force in defense of your life or someone else's, your entire Legal Defense strategy will be based on 'Chance'.

An untrained person who hasn't properly conditioned their minds and their bodies for combat, will experience such an extreme level of stress that they are much more incline to 'Freeze' due to the Shock & Awe effect of the incident. The

- 7 -

only thing 'Freezing' does is make you an easier target to shoot. You must already have a solid understanding of both the 'dynamics' and the 'science' of conflict. Simply knowing how to 'shoot' isn't good enough. This understanding must also be accompanied with sound instinctive fighting habits, gained from quality Procedural Memory Encoding. Then you must amalgamate these into practical, reliable and repeatable fighting tactics. Essentially, you must have a completely Tactical Squared Response allowing you to play Chess while your attacker is stuck playing Checkers.

What are tactics good for if you don't know when you can use them? Too often Armed Citizens place themselves in some of the most legally compromising of situations due to a complete ignorance to the laws associated with Self-Defense. Without this knowledge, your complete tactical defense is a crapshoot based solely on your ability to make 'reasonable' decisions in the heat of battle. You will soon learn how impossible a task that is. Don't rely on 'chance', become a student of Self-Defense Law and base your tactical response on a firm legal foundation.

Hands down the most overlooked aspect of Firearms Self-Defense, is what comes next. What happens after that deadly encounter is much costlier than most people realize. In fact, even the most 'justified' use of Self-Defense can be found to be 'negligent' in Civil Wrongful Death suits, costing victims millions of dollars all for defending their lives from vicious attackers. What you require is a Proactive Legal Defense which becomes the foundational 'rock' your Tactical Response is built on. The best solution for a solid Proactive Firearms Legal Defense is the *ZuluShield System*, which doesn't only offer the most practical approach to such a defense, but it's the best way of insulating one's legal defense, making it a bulletproof defense which can withstand even the most extreme court battles.

The intent of this book focuses on the first aspect of a bulletproof Tactical Response, 'Sound Combative Training'. How though, does one determine which training, tactics and equipment are most effective and practical for real-life gun battles? Which training methods provide the most "bang for your buck," (pun entirely intended), and which methods are most practical and useful for a real-life armed confrontation? If given a choice to be privately trained on how to shoot a basket by the worlds best player of all time; Michael Jordan or by Joe the Builder; who was the star point guard on his seventh grade AAU team, which would you choose? When considering the deadly consequences of losing a gun battle, would you pick a method of combat that looks good on paper? Or would you rather choose a tried, tested and proven method employed by elite tacticians who define the Art of Combat?

Man was not born with a gun in hand. However, many have died with one, simply because they were taught the wrong ways to use them. We do not have the natural ability to shoot well let alone with pure accuracy under fire. This takes a ton of training. However, it's more about the RIGHT kinds of training.

In terms of effectiveness, consistency, accuracy and lethality, there's no argument. The best of the best belongs to the ultra secretive community called Special Operations. DELTA, Navy SEALs, Special Forces, MARSOC, AFSOC, Army Rangers and SWAT. These are but a few of the organizations who belong to this secretive society. These are the elite, the practitioners of warfare and the masters of conflict. Yet surprisingly, their tactics and methods are rooted in simplicity, practicality and repeatability.

Would you like to learn the secrets behind how members of the Special Operations community use their weapons and exactly how the achieve such a high degree of accuracy under the most extreme levels of stress? Are you interested in discovering the most scientifically proven methods of firearms mastery? How about a process of firearms training which not only saves you time and money, but can be performed virtually anywhere with no ammunition requirement and no trips to a firearms range? Are you interested in a system capable of providing you with the ability to not only shoot your firearms with superb accuracy, but also enables you to master all of its parts, accessories and the overall use of it, to include reloads and malfunctions? If so, this system will prove to be of great importance and an invaluable resource. The intent of the following chapters is to communicate both the reality and dynamics of Firearms Self-Defense, combined with an exploration into the science behind this most controversial topic, followed by the most practical and effective Firearms Total Training System so you can fight and win with confidence.

As a product of the dangerous streets of 1980's West Chicago, I learned firsthand the most important lessons of survival. The average American, or really anyone who comes from what we term as being 'The West', lives their lives believing laws, morals, values and common courtesies actually protect and sustain our peace-filled existence of 'Freedom'. This couldn't be further from the truth. Truth is, that which protects and sustains our mortal existence has more to do with intellect and preparedness and much less to do with justice or common values. In fact, the most vulnerable individuals to mortal defeat by the hands of another are not those who live in places like war torn Darfur. The most vulnerable among us are the average everyday 'Westerner' who grows up in a society which conditions them into a false sense of security and reality. It's the individual who wakes up in the morning, goes about their day and later lays down their head at night, without ever once contemplating one all important reality at least once that very day. It's the person who can live their lives day to day, without ever cognitively thinking that someone may actually attempt to kill them that day, they are the 'vulnerable' ones.

Life is not guaranteed. To protect life and freedoms, one must first prepare and then always be aware. Each and every day, good people die at the hands of prowling wolves that lurk in seek of easy prey. I learned to always be prepared and always be ready to act. I learned the difference between 'Existing' vs. 'Living'. Simply existing is a most passive, inactive and unguided state of being. Living, "the act of living," begins with the understanding that life is active and therefore must be perfected and protected in order to sustain it. You see, the only assurance of peace, freedom and life, is found in one's own ability to identify particular vulnerabilities in their individual daily lives, analyze the probability to determine susceptibility, then preplan contingencies to counter an attack. Street Smarts... it saves millions of proactively aware citizens multiple times a day, every day.

ZuluFight is much more than words on paper. It's a looking glass into the science behind armed conflict. The intent of this system is to educate the reader while also providing the best means for perfecting one's craft. It's not intended to magically turn you into a Navy SEAL. However, it will teach proper technique rooted in both a factual and practical understanding of armed confrontation. The winning combination of an effective Tactical Response is only gained through a dedication of time by honing and polishing one's technique. Sure you could fast forward the pipeline of mastery by shooting ten-thousand rounds a week like an Operator. However, you're not an Operator and doing so will actually cause you to miss the mark all together by encoding poor technique.

Operator's first encode proper fundamental mechanics long before they achieve firearms mastery. When they go to the range, their goal is 'perfect precision'. Each and every round fired is fired with an obsessed focus on utilizing 'perfect' fundamentals to afford them an unheard of degree of precision there by further installing 'perfect' technique every time. You won't find them plinking, they shoot with a purpose and their purpose is to train to win, no exceptions. However, the average armed citizen doesn't have the privilege of participating in a Special Operations raining pipeline. The average citizen is greatly limited by both rescore and proximity to the extreme caliber of individual instruction the average Operator receives. The average citizen's level of overall mastery will never be that of a member of SOF; however, it is entirely possible to learn how to be just as lethally competent in a close quarters firearms use. It comes down to how well you train and how well you master the fundamental mechanics of combative firearms use.

The master of tactical strategy, Sun Tzu, once said "Every battle is won before it's ever fought." These words couldn't ring more true. The fact is, when discussing the subject of combat, two mortal beings engaged in a struggle for life itself, two overwhelming facts determine all. First, whose plan is better crafted and secondly, who's able to carry out their strategy with the highest proficiency? Yet, it's also been said: "No battle plan survives first contact." To this, the naive press forward and rely on their utter lack of experience in hopes 'Chance' may save them. It's the supreme warrior who plans, strategies, prepares and plans again. The skilled warrior becomes the enemy and fights his battle a thousand times before he's even met his adversary.

In these uncertain times, thousands of Americans have lost trust in both our Public Safety and Judicial system's ability, or shall I say inability, to protect us from violent criminals. Hence, many have opted to arm themselves with the intent to use their weapons and stand their ground in self-defense. In fact, for the first time in our history, numerous law enforcement officials across America are advising citizens to arm themselves due to such an uptick in violent crimes combined with the likelihood that Cops won't respond in time to save their lives.

Is it that simple though? Simply arming yourself in no way prevents a dangerous criminal from attacking you. Firearms aren't secret cloaks and they're not a form of anti-criminal kryptonite. They don't have secret powers. Moreover, the effective use of a firearm in self-defense is a daunting task to say the least. It requires much more than accuracy. Neither is it about being the quickest draw. Using a weapon in self-defense is combat, a word almost exclusively associated with military operations, not every day citizens. Self-Defense with a weapon is combat and combat is the most fluidly violent unforgiving environment in which one could ever find themselves. Knowing how to use your firearm in Self-Defense is vital. However, even more importantly, knowing how to use your firearm with mastery is your best chance of surviving an actively aggressive, mortally combative, violently attacking threat to your mortal being. ZuluFight will help achieve this goal.

It wasn't the sword that made the Samurai. It was the Samurai's ability to present an impenetrable defense combined with an overwhelming offensive using all manner of skill and weaponry. The Samurai was just as deadly with his sword as he was with an improvised weapon randomly employed during the heat of battle. It's not the weapon that defines a warrior. It's the warrior's ability to accurately decipher his threat and instantaneously present a defense, while simultaneously introducing his offensive, through the effective utilization of the tools he has at hand, combined with the tactics of his craft.

The intent of ZuluFight is to educate the trainee on the most scientific approach to Firearms Self-Defense. The outcome is up to you. Responding successfully during an armed confrontation takes a massive amount of time and training. ZuluFight provides the warrior with the best way to perform said training while also educating them on the real dynamics they will face. Most people foolishly take to the range thinking that by shooting thousands of rounds they will somehow become masters of combat. Practice makes perfect right? Well... poor practice makes widows every day.

Actively dedicating real effort to this system, setting aside time once or twice a week is all that's needed. ZuluFight will turn your inabilities into firearms mastery. First commit to the mastery of your firearm. Next, study this system in its entirety. Refrain from the urge of eating your desert first. Don't skip to the exercise sections at the back of this book before thoroughly reading the chapters which precedes them. A comprehensive understanding of the concepts and science behind Firearms Self-Defense and the methods of this system, are extremely important.

You may find some of these concepts to be controversial especially when considering the topic of gun-sight use. My advice is to study the following chapters with an attention to detail. While doing so, think through the concepts and learn why they make more sense. After that it's time to train. It's important to train with a purpose and dedication to perfecting fundamental mechanics, it's not about racing your way through to the end. Test it out, give it a try but do so with an open mind. Dedicate yourself to a minimum of one month of ZuluFight training. Perform at least one ZuluFight session each week. Do so with the utmost focus and attention to detail. After that, test your skill at the range.

Your quest for mastery begins at home. Tomorrow's deadly attack is overcome before you meet your adversary. Discover how to be just as surgical with your firearm as an SOF Operator. Learn how to win tomorrows battle today. Train today so you're ready tomorrow!

1
Fighting To Win

"Sending a thousand rounds down range poorly, is an extremely expensive way to learn to do something wrong."
—Instructor Zulu—

    The difference between 'Frosted Flakes' and 'Wheaties' is that Wheaties is the better balanced, healthier option. Toyota didn't invent the car. However, with the creation of the Prius, they've given us a more efficient way to drive a car. I haven't reinvented the wheel and I don't claim to be the founder of 'Dry-Fire Training'. What I offer is a better way to perform said training while also insuring a scientifically proven, instantaneous response, that actually works in the real-world. I'm providing you a more tactically sound approach that's based on the 'Science' of conflict.

    One of the most closely held secrets of the Special Operations Community is the quintessential differences between how they employ and use firearms and tactics compared to how the rest of the military use their weapons. Have you ever wondered how Navy SEALs, Special Forces and others in this ultra secret community of elite warriors, acquired such laser focused accuracy? I mean how is it that a 20-year-old MARSOC Operator with only two years of total military experience, is able to completely outshoot an Infantry Gunnery Sergeant with over 20-years military experience as though the Gunny had just graduated Boot Camp? The answer is actually very simple. The difference is in the particular method and manner in which the SOF Community trains. Even in the most daunting and stressful of environments, that contrasting difference affords a SOF Operator the ability to acquire such a superb level of firearms accuracy, which looks like super hero black magic.

    ZuluFight is best described as being a Firearms Total Training System. It addresses every aspect of firearms use; both physiologically and psychologically, to assure an instantaneous kinesthetic response. In terms of methodology, the most scientifically sound way to learn a kinesthetic process is through Procedural Memory and Muscle Memory Encoding. Most shooters are completely unaware of the extreme benefit and importance this type of training offers when it relates to firearms use for defensive purposes.

Dry-Fire Training is an example of this. Traditional Dry-Fire Training is nothing new, it's been used by many tactical professionals and competitors for a number years. However, Traditional Dry-Fire training methods plagued with systemic hazards which unintentionally place the trainee at considerable disadvantage during real-world deadly encounters.

ZuluFight is a scientifically based training system, providing much more than firearms accuracy. It is firearms mastery through Procedural Memory. Most importantly, it is more than simply training; it is a dedication to a whole new lifestyle and mindset. This system conditions your brain to innately and instantly respond to threats without hesitation and or thought. It's also specifically designed to give you the best method of mastering everything related to firearms use including those annoying malfunctions with WILL occur at the precise moment you can't afforded it. The daily and or weekly practice of this system, conditions your psyche to expect attack and prepare beforehand, in order to immediately counter such an attack with the highest probability of success.

One cannot learn proper shooting mechanics through simply shooting. Why? Recoil. Even the most experienced shooters struggle with recoil anticipation. Recoil combined with poor technique is the worst kind of tactical toxin one could ever ingest. It's not until one masters the basic mechanics of the 'Act' of shooting, when the presence of recoil has a limited effect. Sending a thousand rounds down range poorly, is an extremely expensive way to learn to do something wrong.

Firearms are actually very simple when it comes to how they operate. It can be watered down to one simply depressing the trigger in the proper manner while at the same time assuring that they are also employing other important fundamentals like proper stance, grip and follow-through. As long as the firearm itself is in proper order, it will do the same exact thing every time the trigger is fully depressed. It's the shooter who determines where the round will hit.

As a Sniper, I was introduced to the magical benefits of dry-fire practice. I say magic because in comparison to what many do, this most simple and inexpensive technique makes all the difference. Being an expert Sniper is much more than simply shooting well, it truly is an all encompassing craft of tactical warfare, involving much, much more than depressing triggers and calling wind. For the purposes of this though, I will focus solely on the shooting aspects of Sniping.

The particular type of shooting a Sniper employs is by far the most perishable of all firearms skill sets. This means a Sniper's degree of accuracy is completely depended upon his or her overall extent and scale of dedication to training. Putting environmental and geophysical factors aside, the difference between an expert rifleman and a Sniper comes down to 'Finesse'. It's in the Sniper's methodically subtle, delicate manor of utilizing the perfection of body mechanics, through the highest degree of technique, that makes their trigger depresses so lethally accurate and final.

However simply going to the range to learn how to finely hewn one's technique behind a rifle is impossible. Yes, one could easily extrapolate the outcome down range, you either hit or missed. However, what if you're craft is in the art of splitting hairs. How can one determine supreme accuracy down range when the units of measurement are sub-minutes-of-angle (MOA)? The average citizen might take a trip to the range and be so overjoyed that three out of five rounds touched at one-hundred yards. Heck, they may even post a picture of it on Facebook to show the masses.

Yet at this range a Sniper would walk away completely pissed-off if they didn't see a dimed sized or smaller hole exactly where they were aiming. A Sniper knows that if he can see his misses at a hundred yards, he hasn't a chance in Hell of hitting his target at a thousand yards. So he trains and trains and trains. But how does the Sniper measure such minute variances of point-of-aim vs. point-of-impact if all you can see on the target afterwards, is one big hole? The answer is simple; he already did before sending the next round. The Sniper has already called his shot based on their ability to self-coach. They knew while depressing the trigger if they did so with the proper degree of technique. He or she may have depressed with too much force or too much grip, and in turn realize just as the trigger is depressed, that the round will hit down one quarter inch or up one half. They learn this through hours and hours and hours of multiple trigger squeezes. They do so through a technique called 'Snapping-in' or Dry-Fire Training. This is where they can mentally focus on the mechanics of each trigger squeeze completely absent the distractive overload of recoil.

A Sniper's rifle has an extremely limited lifespan in comparison to that of the average handgun or even tactical rifle. It boils down to number of rounds down tube. Our rifles degrade with each passing round. For instance, my duty sidearm has easily over a million rounds to its name. I've never had to replace or repair anything besides a few well used magazines. However, the average Sniper Rifle has a life span of only a few thousand rounds tops before its barrel becomes a liability. So the idea of shooting tens of thousands of rounds in hopes of obtaining perfection with a rifle, is not only an expensively exhaustive endeavor but it's about as feasible as attempting to summit Mt. Everest wearing only Speedos, you WON'T make it.

Ninety-nine point nine percent of firearms inaccuracy relates to poor body mechanics on the part of the shooter. It boils down to how well one is able to manage the particular ways in which the shooter marries all their movements into perfect technique. Measuring extreme accuracy is more accurately accomplished before recoil even happens. It's best done by determining the level of perfection one has in the implementation of physical movement, while being certain not to move their weapon in the course of said movement. How does one learn this? It's accomplished the very same why a Sniper does through Dry-Fire Training.

I like to compare this to how one learns to drive safely at high speeds. Before you learn to drive safely under speed one must first learn the kinesis of driving. We've all driven behind a Driver's Ed car in traffic as they attempt to maneuver around a corner. Their movements are choppy with a lot of back and forth jerking and an abundance of excessive breaking combined with an inconsistent balance of speed management. However, over time they learn to use physics and allow centrifugal force to pull them around the corner. They learn when to take their foot off the gas, why not to brake excessively, the proper amount of turn input and when to place their foot back on the gas and just how much acceleration is needed to accomplish a perfect turn.

However even the average experienced adult driver has no clue as to how to drive safely at high speeds. Yeah sure, you may be comfortable driving at 70 or even 80 MPH but when Old Man Rain makes the roads slick or Grandma Sally decides to randomly cut you off, your inexperience at speed my just get you killed.

Defensive shooting is like speed-racing at speeds well over 150 MPH. To learn how to drive competently at these speeds, one must first learn to be proficient in mastering the fundamentals of driving at speeds between 0-60 MPH. The basic driving techniques are the same between 0-60 and 150 MPH. It comes down to how well a person perfects their technique; the 'Finesse', that makes the difference in a race and that finesse is acquired by mastering those fundamentals at much lower speeds.

The very same is true in the mechanics of shooting. Dry-Fire Training is how one learns the proper techniques required in combat when they're racing against their enemy and time at speeds well over 150 MPH. By perfecting and mastering their skill at lower speeds in training, they have the best chances of winning the race tomorrow. Dry-Fire Training also insures that when you finally go to the range you're not wasting gas, or in this case precious and very expensive ammunition. Snapping-in is how a Sniper spends their off-time; it's how they learn to feel their trigger, and its how their body learns to marry their rifle so it's another extension of themselves. Their range-time is only useful once they've perfected the art of shooting at low speeds.

It's this same level of perfection that separates SOF Operators from shooters. ZuluFight won't make you a DELTA FORCE Operator. However, it will help you master fundamental firearms mechanics and technique. It provides you with a method of perfecting your craft without sabotaging it through poor training. ZuluFight introduces you to the dynamics surrounding armed confrontation while also providing you with a cookbook formatted training regimen; that if followed, assures maximum Procedural Memory Encoding over any other training system.

At a glance ZuluFight may appear to be old hat. However, an objective valuation shows you just why ZuluFight is your healthier more balanced option. Through painstaking reengineering Traditional Dry-Fire Training methods, I was able to identify and isolate extremely troubling methods of practice which simply didn't translate to a 'Win' in combat. Using science as a measuring line, ZuluFight gives you a more probable solution. The most obvious and fundamental difference between ZuluFight and other Traditional Dry-Fire training comes down to the use of gun sights. Making adjustments on how and when to use your gun sights in training, teaching yourself to use them in a way that's scientifically balanced, is what makes all the difference tomorrow. While this may not appear to be a critical divergence, the following chapters will clearly articulate just how significant such an adjustment actually is.

Aside from the drastic differences in the use of gun sights, ZuluFight is better polished and has the overall fit and finish of a luxury car. This gives the trainee a more complete end product. Traditional Dry-Fire training methods focus on trigger manipulation. ZuluFight was designed to include everything from basic operation to clearing malfunctions, holster use, stance etc. while also encoding instinctive, subconscious, and psychologically based 'Fight' protocols. It truly is a 'Total Training System'.

It doesn't matter how experienced you are. Similar to other Traditional Dry-Fire methods, ZuluFight maximizes consistency, efficiency and accuracy in the use of firearms by both novices and tactical experts. Like other Traditional Dry-Fire training, it's the easiest most practical and cost effective method of training, requiring zero ammunition and no trips to the range and is done from the comforts of your own home. ZuluFight goes further though. With ZuluFight you end up with better overall outcome, providing you a much more Tactical Squared Response. Other training methods simply can't give you the overall totality of training ZuluFight offers. It's not just trigger presses, it's an all in one approach to mastering all aspects of firearms use including:

- All eight marksmanship fundamentals.
- Component familiarization (safeties, de-cockers, slide-locks etc.)
- Holster and sling use and familiarization.
- Reloading (Combat and Tactical Reloads)
- Malfunctions (Type 1-3)
- Par-time responses.

A concerning trend...

A troubling and overwhelming majority of firearms owners and concealed weapon carriers rarely train with their weapons, let alone with any consistency. When they do train, it's usually unrealistic and or completely impractical for defensive purposes. What's even more troubling is that many actually believe they are capable and proficient enough. Yes, most of us are fooled into thinking that because you were trained by an NRA, law enforcement or even military instructor, that the training methods you've now adopted are actually practical and effective in real-world gun battles. Truth is you couldn't be more wrong.

Being proficient in firearms combatives requires a level of dedication ninety-nine percent of us never come close to. Most of us approach firearms ownership and training with utmost ignorance and with a completely naïve understanding of reality. We bear such dangerous and destructive tools simply because we're told it's our Second Amendment Right. However, when our founding documents were drafted, concepts like the 'Bearing of Arms' meant much more than simple ownership. In our forefathers' days, nearly every household owned firearms. They were an essential tool in a society which not only had to hunt for sustenance, but was also responsible for fending off attack on all sides. To them, the ownership of firearms brought with it the responsibility of safe and prudent use of it. Today however, most people haven't the slightest clue about safe and prudent ownership much less their use.

If you own or are planning on owning firearms, you need to think hard and ask yourself if you truly know how to be safe, prudent and proficient at all times, even under attack. If the answer is yes, rethink. Remember ninety-nine-percent haven't the foggiest idea where to begin. Being responsible requires a commitment and habit of training that's pushed off or ignored by the masses. I'll admit the combination of life's business and the overall cost of ammunition is a huge factor in this. Add to this the fact that firearms ranges are becoming more difficult to find.

However, the Laws of Physics and Nature trump the conveniences of our daily activities. Failure to train translates to a failure to win every time.

Even worse, nearly every armed citizen is completely ill equipped with employing practical tactics, while maintaining combat effective accuracy, during a dynamic and violent struggle for their lives. In fact, the vast majority never put much thought into the dynamics of combat itself. Those that begin such a journey of thought, typically stop short of thinking through the problem and settle on the assumption that they will somehow prevail like Jason Bourne. We watch movies like 'Taken' and foolishly convince ourselves that good always prevails over evil. Through media and video games, we condition our psyche to view combat with a sense of romance. We see it as a sort of sporting event. When we are taken down, a whistle will be blown, allowing us to huddle and re-spawn for an additional three attempts before conceding. We see movies like the 'The Matrix and fool our minds into believing that when we face an armed attack, we'll slow down time, dodge the bullets, and return fire with ease. We even subconsciously believe in the possibility of altering a bullet's path midflight.

Statistics show police officers only have a twenty-percent hit ratio during real-world shootouts. Police officers are professionals who undergo an extreme amount of specialized and regular firearms training. Twenty-percent may be a shock to you, probably because that's not what you see on TV or in the movies. The truth... real-world combat is a fluid, violent and eternally unpredictable. Combat is greatly compounded by the most extreme levels of unimaginable stress. Being able to hit anything under these circumstances is a horribly arduous task, let alone on a violently moving threat.

If you thought things couldn't be worse, they most certainly are. Officer Involved Shootings are almost exclusively reactionary. When an officer fires their weapon, it's almost exclusively following some sort of deadly attack on them. Simply put, it's a reaction. Physics tells us that "Action" is faster than "Reaction," every time.

Here's an analogy of Action vs. Reaction in relation to combat. Most of us as kids made the painful error of placing our hands on a burning hot stovetop. In a very short time of doing so, the radiating heat was sensed by our nervous system which almost instantaneously caused our hand to be violently pulled back towards our body and away from the heat source. However, the damage had already been done, our hand was burned and a very painful lesson learned. Yet in combat, there are no do-overs. It's not a video game; there's no re-spawning in combat. Combat is not the place to learn because the consequences are eternally final.

Understanding this concept and its relationship to an officer's overall response toward a deadly threat is important. The fact that an officer is even capable of returning fire while under attack means they have already prepared for that battle long before it ever happened. So a twenty-percent hit ratio is reasonable. Yet, is there a way to increase this ratio to eight-percent or more?

Compare all this to the average armed citizen. The citizen trains to shoot paper targets. Their preconceptions of what real combat is, are grossly influenced by movies. In comparison to the average police officer's daily life, the average citizen's life operates in an almost ultra state of peace. Sure, they may experience stress, but a Cop expects a gun battle at every traffic stop and every domestic violence call. So imagine for a moment the extreme difference in affect a Deadly Force encounter has in terms of shock to the system, for an officer who's constantly living on the edge with that of the average citizen who's just been completely blindsided. Now ask yourself what your hit ratio would be given these truths. The answer... less than twenty-percent and much closer to zero.

Stop the insanity...

The definition of insanity is doing something the same way while expecting a different outcome. It can also be translated into doing the wrong thing over and over while expecting the right outcome to miracle itself into existence. You could use your head to hammer a nail; but logic would tell you that you will have a massive headache afterwards.

Studies shown that the average human reaction-time is about 0.30 seconds. That's simply to identify an attack and begin the process of formulating or calculating an appropriate response. That is simple reaction-time. However, reacting to a deadly threat causes a slightly different chemical reaction within our brains. Due to the perceived threat to one's actual existence, the average untrained individual will experience an initial 'Shock and Awe' effect, a sort of stunning pause. This creates lag in actual response to a deadly threat. So in reality, studies show it takes an additional 0.53 seconds to overcome the 'Shock and Awe' of such attack and actually begin a physical response. That's 0.83 seconds from when you're attacked until when you're physiologically ready to react. It takes even longer to actually implement the particular response you're brain has selected to counter the attack.

Studies also show the average untrained individual can shoot four rounds in one second using a Glock-style firearm. That's on tests done with college students who've never previously even held much less shot a firearm before. So do the math, if you you're reacting to a threat who's shooting at you, you could feasibly sustain 3.32 gunshot wounds before you're even able to physically respond. The reality is you are likely to sustain between 6.52-10.88 gunshot wounds before you can get your first shot off depending on how you're carrying your firearm. The sad truth is molten hot, razor-sharp, metal objects have torn through your flesh at nearly 1,200 fps causing you to bleed profusely and you've only just started your FIGHT. Now don't you wish you would have spent just a little more time beforehand, preparing for a perfect response?

Shooting paper every few months or so and relying on the hope that you'll perform under fire in the way in which you envisioned in time of peace, sets you up for a very rude and life threatening awakening. Combat is not where you want to learn these lessons. Master Sun Tzu explains that a warrior wins his battles before he's been there, through preparation, strategy and determination. Your ability to effectively overcome a violent attack and deadly action; with a formidable defense and responsive reaction, can only be achieved through proper preparation.

ZuluFight is a no-brainer. It conditions your brain to quickly identify an attack and your body to instantly respond without thought. No timeouts, no re-spawning necessary. This system is your best solution for Tomorrow's deadly encounter when time is something you DON'T have. ZuluFight pre-programs your psyche to maintain awareness at all times, thereby expecting attack, causing you to live your daily life prepared and ready. ZuluFight saves you time and money by providing you a means to perform the highest quality firearms training at no reoccurring cost, no ammunition, no cleaning, and no hassle. You don't even have to worry about the weather, range availability or the cost of gas to drive out to the hills. Simply put, you don't have to take hours out of your limited time off. ZuluFight can be performed anytime, day or night, at home, in the office or even on vacation in your hotel room. Winning tomorrow's battle today is up to you and its achieved first at home.

2

ZuluScience

"He wins his battles by making no mistakes"

— Sun Tzu —

I said it before and I'll keep saying it, Civilian Firearms Self-Defense is no different than military combat. The very same realities exist and the very same outcomes prevail. He who wins, lives, he who loses, dies. Man was not born with a gun in hand. However, many men have died with one simply because they lacked the appropriate understanding of the dynamics of armed conflict and because they were taught ineffective and impractical ways of using firearms. Being effective with a firearm while under attack is an acquired skill set; it's not something you're born with. Being accurate under fire requires a commitment to the study of these dynamics, combined with adherence to an extensive training regimen.

The vast majority of armed citizens approach the idea of defending their lives with a firearm from the most unfortunate false sense of reality. Their perspectives on the subject of Firearms Self-Defense are clouded and completely misguided, altered by a life's long influence of Hollywood action films and the folklore of the Old West style cowboy showdown at high noon. Their perspectives, expectations and assumptions couldn't be further from the truth.

When bullets start flying, the realities, disadvantages, struggles, consequences and overall dynamics of armed confrontation; with an intruder in your home, is no different than a SWAT Hostage Rescue takedown. Defending one's self with a firearm, while engaged in a close-quarters confrontation with a deadly criminal, is no different than a Delta Force shootout with an armed terrorist.

The reality is, bullets don't discriminate they decimate. They can't tell the difference between friend and foe, let alone professional or amateur, victim or criminal. Bullets fly at thousands of feet-per second, slam into and violently tare their way through meaty flesh while causing massive blood lose and impending death. The very same extreme aptitude requirements of a Navy SEAL; when it relates to Close-Quarters-Battles, is just as true for an armed citizen attempting to defend their lives from deadly attack. For this reason, it's paramount that you commit to studying and understanding the dynamics surrounding armed confrontation. Only after this can you develop the essential skills required to successfully defend your life while under direct attack.

Hint, hint...

I'll let you in on a secret. The reason SOF Operators train the way they do, is because they've learned the science behind combat. Some people wrongly assume SOF members learn and employ out-of-this-world tactics. In reality, they become scholars of science, learning streamlined actions and tactics. Instead of attempting to defy the laws of Physics & Combat, they learn to encode practical solutions for real-world attacks.

When you consider which training methods should be used and exactly what tactics one should be employ during a deadly encounter, why attempt to reinvent the wheel? Why settle for anything less than the most effective, practical and scientifically proven training style capable of translating to a 'Win' tomorrow? Your life relies on your response to an immediate threat. You won't have time to contemplate or calculate your response. There are no time-outs. You most likely won't even have the opportunity or the proximity to flee. Your response must be perfect and completely absent even the slightest bit of hesitation. Settling for anything less than a completely squared-away response, may just prove to be the most devastating compromise you'll ever make. Understanding the science behind combat is your best chance of survival.

Sun Tzu tells us that the surest way to win a battle is by making no mistakes. When considering the extreme dynamics pertaining to the 'Act' of combative firearms use and the stresses associated with combat itself, is it even feasible to fight your fight without making errors? I would argue that it is entirely possible but only if the warrior first gains understanding in the 'Science' behind conflict. ZuluFight is established on this science which is commonly known as 'Force Science'. Force Science is the study of the most extreme forms of physical conflict between humans known as Deadly Force Encounters. Force Science dissects the dynamics associated with combat to identify and measure physiological and psychological effects which may be common from one person to another.

So what is it anyway...

Force Science is the study of the most extreme forms of physical conflict between humans known as 'Deadly Force Encounters'. Force Science dissects the dynamics associated with Combat to identify and measure physiological and psychological effects, which may be common from one person to another.

Force Science is a frailly new discipline, which began in the early 1970s. The intent was twofold:

1. The Special Operations Community wanted to find ways to increase a warfighters' overall potency on the battlefield and identify ways to pass this on to the regular army.

2. Top military brass were concerned with the overwhelming number of service members returning from Vietnam, who suffered from extreme psychological disorders. The extremely high numbers of Psych Casualties were most alarming and far greater than any previous conflict. They wanted to figure out what if anything had changed; in

terms of Combat, and exactly how Combat; itself, effected the average warfighter.

The long and short is that scientists found exactly what they were searching for, but they also uncovered a treasure trove of information that's completely changed how we approach Combat today. However, it took some time for scientist, psychologist and doctors to catch up to a whole new way of thinking.

Twenty years later; in the 1990s, two main groups took this research to a whole new level and made it the science we know today. KILLOLOGY RESEARCH GROUP and the FORCE SCIENCE INSTITUTE ® are two completely independent and unbiased-based groups comprised of scientists, doctors, psychologist and tactical experts, who focus on the physiological and psychological effects of Deadly Force Encounters. Man has been in Combat since Cane and Able, yet astonishingly, the 'Science' behind Combat has been pretty much hit and miss, (pun intended) until the advent of the above mentioned groups.

They were the first to connect the dots and fill in the gaps from the more archaic research of the 1970s. They were able to identify patterns and extrapolate probable outcomes to give us a much better understand of exactly what to expect when we're faced with a Deadly Threat. What their research has found tells us that we've been doing it wrong all along. Sadly, we've been training to LOSE not to win.

In search of the Enigma...

Solid combatives training is a key element in any effective Self-Defense Response. To survive the battle, you MUST gain effective proficiency in the 'Kinesis' of the 'Fight'. So how does one determine on method over another and is there a particular method, as a 'Holy Gail' of firearms training which surpasses all the rest? Is there even a such thing? Even if there wasn't some sort of Holy Grail of tactical gurury, I determined there had to be 'Something' better than training to 'Lose'. So my search began. Through years of study, I painstakingly analyzed mounds of data, while comparing multiple firearms training methods. I used Force Science principles as a measuring line to arrive at a more objective valuation between methods. Surprisingly, I learned the vast majority of today's firearms training programs are dangerously faulty and inadvertently sets-up students for mortal failure.

Through the use of Force Science, I was able to uncover a much more practical and scientifically sound method of training. When the dust settled, I had found an approach to firearms combatives training, which far exceeded any another stands alone training method. It's not that my ideas were anything new. I didn't invent some fancy new idea. I simply uncovered a mystery that's only been kept secret because we've been approaching 'Firearms Training' with a perspective that looks good on paper but leaves one attempting to defy 'Physics' when the actually battle arrives. What I discovered was that there actually is a method of training which is superior and more complete, scientifically, than todays typical approach.

Quite honestly my approach was nothing new at all. In fact, its compactly founded on the most basic method of human physical development and utilizes a technique, which is already widely used throughout the Tactical Community. I simply connected the dots, dust off the clutter and went about infusing scientific principles into the Kata of training. By using Force Science as my looking glass, I was able to identify extremely dangerous, systemic hazards, present in many other training methods, so as to 'Cut The Dead Wood' and remove these hazards which attempt to defy science itself. I then filled the gaps, which others methods inadvertently overlook, to arrive a much more well-rounded approach, for an all-in-one training system. Through the amalgamating two tried and tested methods of human learning, I was able to better refine this training concept. One is based on the kinesthetic processes of ancient Martial Arts combatives training. The other key ingredient is based on a handful of scientific theories pertaining to neurological and physiological human development. Both are based in the sciences of physics and physiology and both are completely consistent with the findings of Force Science.

Like many others, I took my training serious. In my eyes, when I trained, I trained for tomorrow's battle. I knew that what I did today would determine tomorrow's outcome. So I considered the plethora of training methods I'd been exposed to in the Tactical Community. Then I thought back on those organizations I'd rubbed shoulders with in training. It didn't take long for me to find my starting point. I had been around a number of amazingly accurate shooters in my years however none could come close to the pure lethality of one particular group, they were by far the best. I wasn't fooling myself, it wasn't as though I thought I could somehow reach their level of overall expertise. It was more about finding out why? Why were they so good, all of them? The obvious answer was training, so what do they do different?

Today's Samurai Warrior is without question the US ARMY 1st SFOD-D aka Delta Force. If you've ever had the privilege of training or operating with them, then you'd know exactly what I mean. You know you've met one when they extend their hand to shake and all you feel is one big callous. Why? I'm sure it has to do with a particular statistic that this group; which is estimated to comprise of only a few hundred elite tacticians, are responsible for shooting over 70% of the U.S. Army's annual total ammunition expenditure. Think about it, a few hundred guys, literally shooting more rounds than nearly 2-million soldiers and reservists combined which also includes their branch's fellow SOF members like Special Forces and Army Rangers. That's pretty remarkable.

It goes without saying that the elite of the elite obviously participate in some pretty high speed tactical sexy training evolutions. However, they have to start somewhere. What I wanted to know is specifically what kinds of firearms training methods they utilize during selection and their 'Operator' training pipeline. What I discovered was that since their birth in the 1970's, the bulk of their firearms training is actually very simplistic. It's not the Hollywood, super trooper, orgy of tactical hoorah, one might imagine. They take an extremely low-drag approach, with increased intensity over extended time spans, with an extreme level of meticulous focus, all the while performing high repetitions. Simply put, they learn to 'See' their target and 'Shoot' their target regardless of the degree of stress stimuli. Sounds simple, see and shoot. However, when introducing stressors, movement, sighting techniques and other related factors, simply seeing and shooting; accurately, is accomplished only through quality, consistence and reciprocation of training.

Dave Ramsey says, "If you wanna be rich, do what rich people do." I'd say the very same is true when it relates to Firearms Self-Defense. If you wanna shoot like the best, train like the best. What Delta Force does with a new recruit is take an already well experienced tactician and focus on polishing up on the building block fundamentals of the 'Kinesis' of shooting. They start out slow and methodically and build up from there. Their streamlined approach phases out inherently poor shooting habits they may have acquired over the years by slowing things down and bypassing useless and time wasting steps and it all based on the repetitious practice of Dry-Fire-Training.

What I did next was to compare the similarities of kinesis to that of the Ancient Martial Arts. When one looks at the meticulous manner in which a martial artist perfects his craft, it's quite evident their goal in training is not speed or even strength. Instead they opt for an almost over-exaggerated slow motion choreographed dance. It's as if they were literally thinking through every millimeter of movement a particular body part makes, in hopes of accomplishing an intended overall orchestra of multiple movements, all playing together in perfect harmony. Considering this, one could easily conclude that Bruce Lee only became the Master of Combative Kinesthesis through slow and deliberate laser-focused, high quality, repetitive movement training. The very same is true for Delta Force Operators. So again if you wanna shoot like a champ, train like one.

Now don't get me wrong, I'm not suggesting ZuluFight; in and of itself, will have you walking away shooting like James Bond. However, with the right degree of focus, a commitment of mastery and through consistent and continued practice, ZuluFight is completely capable of encoding in you, the very same surgical expertise as that of a SOF Operator.

My next task came as a result of my previous study of physiology and brain function. Specifically, I focused on the relationships between Procedural Memory, Kinesthetic Repetitive Conditioning and Muscle Memory Encoding. Procedural Memory has been used synonymously with motor learning, which is a form of muscle memory involving the consolidation of an isolated and specific motor function, tasked into memory through the process of repetitive movement. When an action is repeated over time, a long-term memory is etched into our brain's filing system for that specific task. Over time this process allows said movements to be performed with precision and absent conscious effort.

This is only achieved through Kinesthetic Repetitive Conditioning. Through the process of conditioning, the need for the cognition of a particular movement greatly diminishes, creating a level of maximum efficiency within our brain's motor and memory systems. Examples of the relationship and byproducts of Procedural Memory and Kinesthetic Repetitive Conditioning are found in many everyday activities that become automatic and improve with practice. Tasks such as riding a bicycle, typing on a keyboard, pushing a door bell, are good examples of this, but most notably, speaking, being able to unconsciously communicate without the need to think of the word "The" when saying, "Can you hand me the milk?"

Sounds silly, but something as simple as speaking; which for the most part we all take for granted, is by far the most complex mixture of psychology, physiology and nanophysics, where a contextual cognitive based response is made in relation to our interactions with the world around us. Basically, over years and years of speaking, we get to a point where we end up performing the most complex cognitive based physical response with such precision that we're able to formulate active communication while constantly reacting and adapting said communication for the topic at hand. When we speak, we use 'Thought' or cognition, to calculate what's happened, happening or about to happen, develop a 'Solution' and respond by turning the solution into 'Physical Response', which in this case is speech, that's completely tailored for that unique and specific set of circumstances. When you think about the multitude of all the physical aspects of speech; the movement of the tongue, how one's lips form, the control of the lungs and their exhale which provides the perfect measure of breath that passes through the vocal cords, the placement of the jaw and teeth and the cognitive aspects of what words will be used, you soon realize just how complicated something so simple actually is. We get so good at speaking that we accomplish it all day every day without really having to focus or think about it, through the process of Procedural Memory and Kinesthetic Repetitive Conditioning.

Kata is King:

Your first step towards developing a squared away Self-Defense Response, begins with understanding the composition of Firearms Self-Defense as a whole. Once you've fully grasped the realization, that the act of 'Using' a firearm to defend oneself, requires both a Physical and Psychological process, then you're able to go about honing each aspect with intelligence and an acute attention to detail.

Let's dissect the 'Physical' component or the 'Kinesis' of firearms. Of course, what we all hope for is to somehow acquire an instantaneous response or 'Reflex' to an immediate and deadly threat. Much like the 'Patellar Reflex Test' your doctor does when they tap your knee with that rubber mallet, we hope to develop a defense mechanism that fires immediately upon first contact and hits the mark accurately and without error. Now we all know that nobody is born a fighter or an expert shot, all that is acquired through training. So the obvious question is, which training method is best? When it relates to the kinesis of shooting; the culmination of isolated movements for one overall response, there are a plethora of methods available.

The overall implementation of a firearm's use; during Self-Defense situations, requires a very similar skill-set to that of a Conductor during a feature performance of the worlds greatest orchestra. It relies on one's ability to first tame, then manage a kaleidoscope of multi-faceted individual psychophysical and physiological functions for a completely tailoredmade response, that's performed within the context of the immediate problem at hand.

When it comes to the topic of Firearms Self-Defense, there exists an essential ancient technique of combative training, an elementally crucial ingredient to the 'Craft' of Self-Defense, that is being completely and utterly overlooked by nearly every firearms instructor world-wide. An example of this dying art form can be found in the practice of Japanese Aikido through their concept of 'Kata'. Admittedly, there are a dying few firearms training systems, which involve a hand-full of the methods associated with this ancient practice. However, none of them fully grasp or incorporate the totality of the overall concepts of Combative

Mastery and thus fail to provide the practitioner with a pathway to mastering the Craft of Firearms Self-Defense.

Unfortunately, the vast majority of firearms training methods prove to be counter productive and in many cases actually place the trainee in a much more compromised position than if they wouldn't have even trained at all. Its been said that "Practice Makes Perfect" so many are fooled into believing that if something looks good on paper or the masses support it, then it's got to be worth their time and money. Well, I'd wager that 'Poor Practice' is the fastest way to learn how to lose and in this arena, losing gets you dead. Instead of conditioning appropriate responses, most training methods place the trainee at a disadvantage, where they wind-up wasting time, money and effort, all while conditioning responses, which not only attempt to violate the Laws of Physics, but rely on concepts and movements which are completely impossible to reproduce during an actual real-life fight.

Have you ever wondered how Michael Jordan became the super star he was and still is? During an interview, Jordan claimed that the only way he became so good at his craft was because his mother made him shoot 'Free Throws' every day as child for hours at a time. This concept; 'Free Throws' and its relationship with Firearms Self-Defense is vitally important to grasp.

A Free Throw costs nothing and is a 'Free' attempt at an easy point. As an added bonus, all 'Time' stops and everyone waits for the shooter to concentrate and take his time for two perfect shots. In the NBA, most games often rely on a team's ability to sink these all important 'Free' shots. In any given game you'll see dozens of attempts, where each individual player employs their own unique style. What's different about the Free Throw is the cadence and sequence by which each shooter shoots. As opposed to any other shot, players tend to shoot their Free Throws the exact same way each and every time, time after time, game after game, through their entire careers. You'll notice they each have their own individual way of doing what they do and they do it the same way each time. For instance, a given player will bend their knees and crouch the same way each time. They will bounce the ball in the same manner and the same amount of times prior to the shot. They'll pause for the same amount of time before extending and releasing, in the same manner each and every time.

What's interesting is the manner by which Jordan grew-up practicing his Free Throws. He took this practice to zen-like state of training. He obviously understood the concept of 'Kata'. He polished and honed his shot, so well that in a 1991 game against the Denver Nuggets, he taunted; then rival Dikembe Mutombo, by saying "Hey, Mutombo. This one's for you" He closed his eyes and sunk the shot like nobody's business and followed it up with his pearly whites as he arrogantly smiled back at Mutombo to win the game.

While there might not be some sort of 'Holy Grail', there is a method which far outweighs any of today's more common approaches. At the very least you should invest your time in learning about this approach, adopt its principles and infuse them into your training regime. Dry-Fire Training is to Shooting what the Free Throw is to basketball. If you had to choose (1) method of learning to 'Shoot' and manipulate a firearm, Dry-Fire Training or 'Snapping In' is your BEST choice.

Dry-Fire Training is how one fine tunes and hones their craft and it's the best way to win the fight ahead of time. Dry-Fire Training derives its name from the fact that the trainee presses the trigger on an empty or 'Dry' chamber, meaning there's a complete absence of ammunition. This affords you the ability to practice Trigger Manipulation without the need for ammunition, thereby completely avoiding the need for a firearms range. Just like with basketball Free Throws, all 'Time' stops. You have all the time in the world today, to isolate and perfect each and every individual element, which makes-up the overall movement or function, for that perfect shot tomorrow. You, determine how long it takes to perform said movements and how focused your attention to detail actually is. Best of all Dry-Fire Training is 'Free', can be done from home and is hands down the best way to master one's Kata.

Now I know what you're thinking, how is it possible to learn how to defend one's self with a gun by shooting an empty one at home? Don't you need to master 'Recoil' and actually shoot at targets to know what real bullets actually do? The simple answer is, NO! All bullets do the exact same thing every single time. When the round's primer is struck by the firing pin, the primer initiates a series of controlled explosions, thereby propelling the projectile; or bullet, down the barrel. Once the projectile clears the muzzle, gravity and wind is all that maters. Like bullets, the Recoil of a given caliber of ammunition is the exact same every time in your particular firearm. When the round initiates, physics causes the energy to of the explosion to force the firearm up and back towards you at the very same rate and pitch each and every time. How you go about controlling recoil and sending an accurate round downrange has less to do about shooting and EVERYTHING to do about what you do 'Physically' to the firearm prior to the round ever being fired.

What traditional firearms training does, is attempt to teach a person to learn how to do something 'Right' by first doing something 'Wrong'. What I mean is, they take a novice to a firing range, hand them a loaded firearm, give them verbal instruction on how their supposed to 'Physically' manipulate said firearm, then tell them to "FIRE". What do you think happens? You're right, they miss. Now the instructor goes about attempting to erase the miss through further verbal instruction and has them fire again and again and again until they 'Miss' more accurately. That's what you call learning to do something wrong, expensively.

Some of the best Snipers in history come from Russia. They have consistently produced the deadliest shooters in the greatest numbers since WWI. The reason has to do with 'How' they condition their Snipers. Instead of giving them a box of ammunition and sending them to the range, they spend the vast majority of their time Dry-Firing. Then when the 'Test' comes, they given them ONE round because the first round is the only round that matters.

When a person Dry-Fires a weapon over and over and over, their body begins to 'Feel' its way around the enigma of mastery. Dry-Fire is what breaks the code, while their body feels its way into perfect harmony of that particular firearm's mechanics and its relationship to a given person's own body mechanics. Overtime the two become one and they've become the firearm.

The difference between a Dry-Fire shooter and your typical firearms shooter is that the traditional shooter is forever plagued by recoil. Because the traditional shooter has attempted to learn how to master their firearm under the explosive influence of recoil, they're hands and intern the rest of their body has not been able to 'Feel' the relationship between the perfect grip and trigger squeeze as the firearm is in perfect alignment with their wrists, arms, shoulders and eyes. At any given time the traditional shooter my feel one or two of these find harmony, however the effects of recoil completely prevent them from feeling all of these vital elements at once. However, the Dry-Fire shooter, simply loads their firearm, and manipulates it as though there were no bullet at all. To them what they do; their task, comes 'Before' recoil. Their bodies have memorized how to perfectly feel it's way through the sequence of movements for one harmonious shot.

However, traditional Dry-Fire Training systems fall short and do not provide the totality of training required to master the 'Combatives' of Firearms Self-Defense. Similarly, there are a hand-full of other training methods; like the 'Four Point Draw', which delve into the concepts of Kata, but still fail to provide the density required for an actual fight. However, they also fall short and don't offer a total-training-system like Japanese Aikido. Traditional approaches focus on the 'Movement' but fail to accompany said movement with 'Thought'. The result is a dull blade. Because the trainee hasn't thought their way through the movements, they haven't been able to finely hone or sharpen its edge. Sure a dull edge is better than no edge but wouldn't you rather have the sharpest blade? Traditional Dry-Fire systems also focus on one movement, 'Trigger Presses', and completely fail to incorporate all the other components of Firearms Combatives, like Stance, Grip, Proper Alignment, Follow-Through, Loading & Re-Loading etc. In order to master Firearms Combatives, one must understand the relationship between 'Thought' and 'Kinesis' and amalgamate these into the mastery every aspect of that firearms use.

When you watch a Japanese Aikido master practice his craft, it looks much like a slow-motion choreographed dance. The reason is because he's leaned the magic of marrying thought to movement. When I say 'Thought', I mean laser focused, zen-like concentration. When I say 'Movement' I mean a sloth like slow-motion, over exaggerated, individual and precise sequence of multiple variances. The Aikido warrior becomes a 'Master' of his craft by perfecting the art of 'Thinking Through' his movement's in training, so as to develop a surgically lethal orchestra of combative movement, strategically constructed to embody a given Combative Response for tomorrow's fight. Like a slug on a trail, the Master perfects their art by breaking-down the individual actions of an overall physical response, into minute forms of movement. They then go about polishing each and every individual process to arrive at a perfectly performed kinesthetic response.

To understand this better let's, explore the Japanese concept of 'Kata' which means 'Form' or in other words a particular 'From' of a physical discipline. In Japanese Martial Arts, they believe each physical discipline tells a story and each story can be choreographed into a slow-motion dance and with that dance one can train to 'Master' their discipline.

Kata is based on (3) very important understandings:
1. The 'Structural Integrity' of that discipline.
2. The, 'Coherence' and relationship of the movements required for that discipline.

3. The overall 'Intent' behind that specific discipline.

In terms of Structural Integrity, this discipline is broken up in to a multitude of individually unique movements. Some of these movements are big, while others are small, some of them simple while others are much more complicated, some can be performed quickly while other must be done slowly and with consistent momentum. In the end, the combination of these movements and their orientation to one another, must make sense and one movement must be applicable with the other.

In terms of the Coherence of these movements, everything must flow together to appear to be, one seamless and perfectly performed action. Like water poured from a cup, each individual molecule must be perfectly adhered to the next so that from the outside, it appears the action of fighting is so perfectly complete and intact, that it resembles a cup of water's ability to be poured; which consists of millions of individual water molecules all falling melding together to 'Fall' to the ground as one, at the same speed and in the same fashion.

The Intent of the discipline at hand, speaks for itself. Oddly when it relates to Firearms Self-Defense training, 99% of the methods in existence, completely ignore this all important component. The obvious intent is to 'Kill' your enemy before they kill you. The cognition of the concept of 'Killing' is completely absent at almost every firearms range known to man. Don't get me wrong, most people fully understand the end goal will likely result in someone's death, but the actual cognitive process of the 'Thought' of killing, while practicing each individual movement of shooting, is as foreign a concept on most ranges as Pluto is to Mercury. By focusing on the intent behind the craft while training, knowing that each and every minute movement pertains to the 'Action' of 'Killing' your Threat and that the ability to 'Kill' your Threat is, completely dependent upon the combination of the overall Structural Integrity of your action and its Cohesive qualities to each particular movement, requires one to take their training to a whole new level of consciousness. Its only then that a person is able to Master their Combative Response through the management of their movements.

A Tactical Squared Response...

The next step was to find the best way to perform Dry-Fire Training. To do this I needed to develop a control by which I could accurately evaluate each system. The basis of the control was founded one the concept of the Four Stages of Competence:

1. Unconscious Incompetence

2. Conscious Incompetence

3. Conscious Competence

4. Unconscious Competence

The greatest disadvantage in combat is the required urgency to counter with a physical response that's not only tailored for that specific occasion, but that's also performed with precision and within an extremely limited par-time window.

Thus a cognitive-based physical response; which requires an enormous amount of thought, has only one probable outcome, which is complete mortal defeat. However, an unconsciously precise response offers the highest yield of survivability. I condensed this down to a simple tactical mathematic equation I call a 'Tactical Squared Response'.

Tactical Squared Response:

EM = T Squared

(Efficiency of EFFORT multiplied by Efficiency of MOTION = Response)

I determined the product of 'Tactical Squared' must equal zero. This represents the intended par-time or time it takes to respond to a threat, measured by seconds of response to an imminent deadly threat to one's mortal being. With this being said, the rest becomes a simple algebraic expression. Solve for zero. So either 'Effort' or 'Motion' must also equal zero. In combat, the only way to win is to fight and the only way to fight is to move. So if one must 'Move' to 'Fight' and if one must 'Fight' to 'Win' then 'Motion' can NOT equal zero. The answer to a "Tactical Squared Response" is to use zero 'Effort' while executing utter proficiency in the economy or finesse of 'Motion'. So is it possible to respond physically absent any effort at all? Of course not! However, it is entirely possible to achieve defensive firearms mastery through the most minimal degree of 'Effort' preformed for an Unconsciously Competent response. What it boils down to is the proper management of overall movement. But what about when you add stress and when I say stress, I mean Combate Stress.

Combat Gravity...

If there is one thing the study of Force Science has revealed, it would be that there exists a myriad of unavoidable and common effects, which everybody experiences. Combat itself has a very distinct impact on how a person will actually physically respond while threatened. This impact is vastly different than how a person acts under ANY other circumstances, other than during the most extreme life or death situations. The sum of these effects represent what I call the 'Laws of Combat'. These laws can be likened to Sir Isaac Newton's 'Laws of Physics'. The mere existence of Combat, has a measurable and defined affect on man. Regardless of race, nationality, gender or physical composition, there are a handful of common effects of Combat, which cannot be averted.

Think of it in terms of 'Gravity'. Everybody knows the affect of gravity when it relates to our ability to maneuver here on Earth. It's what keeps our feet to the ground, our constant. In the same way, Combat has its own gravitational force. There are physiological and psychological realties that affect every man, woman or child who experiences Combat.

The reality is that we all experience extremely similar effects during a struggle for our existence. While each individual effect is not guaranteed, every human being engaged in Combat, will experience the majority of them to one extreme or another. While these effects are completely unavoidable, their influence can be dramatically reduced to a much more manageable degree. Science has shown that we can pre-condition our minds and in turn our bodies; beforehand, to experience 'Combat Gravity' with less overall affect on our ability to navigate its waters.

An analogy of this concept can be derived from the conditioning an Astronaut undergoes prior to their travel into outer space. Over a life of experiencing the effects of Gravity here on Earth, their bodies have developed their own harmonic balance. If abruptly thrust into space and placed on the Moon, a person would experience great discomfort and fear without proper preparation, since they would end up bouncing from one side to the other. To this day Astronauts practice simulated Low Gravity Training, so they're adequately prepared for the effects of said Gravity on the Moon or Space in general. Something as simple as drinking water in Space, can be a very daunting task and extremely difficult to complete while in Space. Yet on Earth this most basic function, which most of us master by the age of (4), is taken for granted here on Earth. Similar basic physical functions associated with using a firearm while under attack, are just as much an out-of-this-world experience as drinking water from a cup, in an almost zero gravity environment like that of the International Space Station.

Just as the Moon is a world away from our experiences here on Earth, Combat is as distant our everyday lives as Mars or better yet Pluto. In the same way, Force Science has shown that anyone can prep for tomorrow's battle and develop natural responses to afford them the most positive outcome.

An example on how poor training can completely sabotage one's ability to win during the 'Act' of Combat, can be found in something as simple as how they stand during training. Stance is one of the most overlooked aspects of firearms training, yet it provides the entire base for your Physical Response. For the most part people initially acquire a stance that looks tactical cool like the 'Isosceles Stance'. But soon and usually within a few short minutes, their stance becomes more of a flat-footed, weight on heals Weaver Stance. What happens is they lose focus of the 'Crouch' and forward lean required for an effective Isosceles Stance and quickly get tired due to muscle fatigue. What results is the entirety of the rest of their training is performed from a completely different base, which completely effects overall accuracy. The laziness and poor habitual manner of their stance in training, is then encoded in their brain as Muscle Memory through the procedural aspects of their training.

Interestingly, Force Science research clearly shows that EVERYONE who actually perceives an immediately attacking lethal threat, will instinctively assume a squatted crouch, identical to that of the Modified Isosceles shooting stance. No matter how well you've training and no matter how elite your profession may be, this is latterly an innate physical reaction that CAN'T be overridden. A great example of this can be seen in the video footage of then President Reagan's attempted assassination on March 30th 1981. During this real-world deadly attack EVERY single individual is seen assuming an 'Oh Shi Crouch' directly proceeding John Hinckley Junior's initial shots.

What's even more interesting is that each and every person immediately present did the same exact thing regardless of their previous training or their current physical responsibility. From reporter, to staff, to regular police officers to the elite team of Reagan's Secret Service Detail, each and every person crouched and maintained that crouch throughout their following Physical Response. Remember, members of a Secret Serve Presidential Security Detail, undergo a degree of unheard of pre-training and continued training that could easily be likened to the practice of a Religion. Even with all their training, each Secret Service member crouched in the same fashion and even paused for about the same amount of time, prior to putting into motion their Defensive Response.

The reality is that during attack you WILL assume a 'Modified Isosceles Stance' throughout the incident regardless of your previous training. If Force Science has proven that this is as much of a reality as Gravity is to the Law of Physics, then why do so many people waste so much time shooting from a Weaver or any other type of shooting stance? Your shooting stance is your 'Base' it determines and galvanizes the overall integrity of all other aspects of fighting which shooting is but 'One' portion. Maintaining proper stance through the entirety of your training will assure that all the other physical movements you hone during that training evolution, are not wasted and are built on a sure foundation that's consistent with the Laws of Combat and don't attempt to defy the Laws of Physics. Understanding something so simple yet so vitally important as 'Stance' during training, highlights just why an adequate grasp of the topic of Force Science is so essential if you want to 'Win' tomorrow's battle. Winning is first accomplished through the 'pre'-study of conflict.

The mind, a terrible thing to waste...

Our brains define us and set us apart from all other living beings. The totality, function and overall capabilities they offer are inconceivable. Neuroscientists are still uncovering the secrets and wonder behind how our brains develop and function. Our brains are truly our greatest asset. Yet, in times of great crisis they can often become our greatest obstacle.

Force Science researchers have consistently shown that our ability to manage 'Combat Stress' is directly derived from how our minds process the concepts of this stress beforehand. It's all about pre-conditioning. In fact, our success is completely dependent upon our mind's ability to formulate an instantaneous response absent cognitive thought. Just as our brain's continually cause our lungs to expand and contract without thought, so too must we have a pre-wired solution for tomorrow's battle. This starts by understanding the processes of our physiology and psychology and how they're affected during Combat. Similar to how an Olympic Athlete utilizes Hyperbaric Chamber Training to pre-condition their lungs for the extreme stressors of such a high level of competition. So too, you must pre-condition the physiology and psychology of your mind for Combat.

Fight, Flight or Freeze...

Over the course of our lives, our brains have subconsciously developed one of three instantaneous responses to an immediate and Deadly Threat. We will either 'Fight' our Threat with all our might, 'Flee' from it as fast as humanly possible or we will completely shut down and 'Freeze' like a deer caught in the headlights. This is also known as 'Combat Paralysis', which can last anywhere from seconds or minutes and can easily lead to a medical state of shock.

Our brains are designed to develop and operate on two parallel planes. During times of grave danger and when faced with a threat to our very existence, our brains revert back to the most primitive forms of function.

1. The first and most common plane, I like to call the 'Intelligent Brain'. It's where we live 99.99% of our lives. It's the cognitive and intellectually creative form of us. This operation is achieved through the cooperative interaction of our Prefrontal Cortex with both our brain's right and left hemispheres.

    - To better understand this, our Intelligent Brain is like our desktop computer. It's comprised of all that makes our computer different than the next. It is made up of its operating system and background functions, the main hard-drive, auxiliary drives and the multitude of custom software suites.

2. The second is much more primitive than the Intelligent Brain. I call this the 'Caveman Brain' or the Amygdala. It's mainly comprised of all our basic body functions; the innate processes our brain makes on its own, which maintain all 11 basic body function systems, like those of our nervous and circulatory systems. It also consists of an extremely small sampling of our Intelligent Brain's ability to problem solve.

    - To better understand this, our Caveman Brain is like our desktop computer's master default, the archaic DOS or C Prompt. No Windows OS, no software, just code.

    - Many so called Tactical Experts have training methods which fall apart during real-life Combat because they designed their methods on an Intellectual footing requiring the use of one's 'Intelligent' cognitive brain function. However, during the polar shift of Combat; where our brains revert back to Caveman function, all those 'Intellectual' possesses go out the window. In Combat you're left with basic computer code, while all those fancy dancy high-tech tactical sexy software applications end up crashing. What you should be doing is learning to be a Combat Computer IT Analyst because that's exactly what you'll need when someone tries to kill you tomorrow and you're faced with the complexities of the unavoidable Combat Computer Code Crash.

Due to genetics and early childhood influences, our Caveman Brains accumulate a mixture of automated responses which are immediately fired when faced with grave danger. This is that small sampling of intellectual problem solving discussed above. When faced with a problem our Caveman Brain throws an extremely primitive solution at it. It really is basic Addition & Subtraction though; it's nowhere near the level of Trigonometry or even Basic Algebra. These automated, pre-programmed, responses are completely innate and instinctive. They're an instantaneous function requiring almost zero cognitive processing whatsoever.

Similar to our body's homeostasis; how it regulates and maintains the perfect PH balance, our brains develop their own form of psychoneuro-homeostasis. Over a lifelong of external influences and experiences, our brains establish a physiological and physiological balance. When balanced, this state of being enables our

Intelligent Brains to function with ease in relation to the world around us. However, when faced with impending death, this balance is violently thrown upside-down. At that moment our Caveman Brain floods our systems with a cocktail of the most potent hormones and chemicals. The effects of this mind altering chemical cocktail greatly affects our body's response to the perceived Threat and ultimately determines our overall ability to respond to the Threat(s) or whether we Fight, Flee or end-up Freeze.

Top Secret...

When faced with a Deadly Threat to our very existence, our brains feverishly search for a folder titled 'Top Secret'. This folder holds the solution to our immediate problem. The trouble arises when our brains experiences the polar shift; mentioned previously, as it goes from using the Intelligent Brain to our primitive Caveman Brain. It's at that moment when our secretary; our brain's Amygdala, grabs the first folder she can get her hands on and throws it at the problem. The probability that she will retrieve the particular individual folder, which contains your specifically tailored solution for that particular problem, is completely dependent upon how you've already organized, correlated and filed that folder beforehand. When it comes to the use of a weapon in response to an attacking threat; how you respond, is completely depended upon the degree and quality of Procedural Memory Encoding you've performed beforehand.

Our brains are like huge storage vaults capable of storing a life's long accumulation of information and experiences. For the most part we organize these banks of information in similar fashion to that of a filing system. For Combat experts, this system is as sophisticated as the vault like industrial catalogs like those you'd find at a courthouse or museum.

Most people however, file their information in a much less technical manner. This would more closely resemble an everyday two drawer filing cabinet. Over time our brains develop habits of storage, utilizing different kinds of coding and correlating. Some folders are red while others are blue. Some folders go to the top drawer while others live in the bottom. Some are situated to the left while others are stored to the right. In an everyday world; while experience everyday experiences with low stress, your Intelligent Brain can typically locate nearly any folder by memory of where it was last stored. This is due to the process of Cognitive Thought, which is the brain's overall cooperative effort of all its parts.

Ninety-nine point nine-nine percent of Westerners live their lives in an ultra state of peace. In fact, most Westerners will go a lifetime without being physically confronted let alone have someone actually try and kill them. It's important to understand this because just as our Intelligent Brain develops habits of process, our Caveman Brain does as well. The brain is a muscle and like any muscle, if it's not used, it becomes weak. The down side to our peace filled lives is that our Caveman Brain hardly if ever gets its workout in. So when death comes knocking, our Amygdala is left with the daunting task of finding that 'One' perfect solution for an out-of-this-world problem, amongst the clutter of all the other files, piled up around her. This is where the right kind of training makes all the difference and is precisely why the 'Right' kind of training is so essential.

Our Intelligent Brain utilizes the vastness of the Prefrontal Cortex; which is about the size of your fist, to calculate its solutions for the world around it. In contrast, our Caveman Brain uses an area the size of a pea, the Amygdala. That tiny, barely legible portion of the otherwise vastness of the rest of our brain, that's what our Caveman Brain uses to formulate its response to a Deadly Encounter. That tiny, insignificant dot is the most significantly momentous apparatuses in your entire body. This is what WILL determine how you respond to Deadly Threats. Placing the 'Right' information in an appropriately marked folder during training and storing it in the proper spot, that's what will make all the difference tomorrow. It's this tiny portion of our brain; the Amygdala, that has become the focal point of Force Science. It's this extremely miniscule region of the human brain which gets all the attention. Your ability to overcome tomorrow's Deadly Threat is dependent upon how well you understand this process and how well you 'Condition' and encode a pre-programmed response. Proper conditioning is only achieved through proper training. However, it's not just about 'Training' but the 'Right' kind of training makes this possible.

Most of us place the cart before the horse. We spend a small fortune on that perfect gun, which by all means is guaranteed to stop any bad guy dead in his tracks, right? Wrong! From time to time we set out on a pilgrimage to Tactical Mecca, where we hewn and ready our hands for battle by plinking at cardboard silhouettes or even glass bottles. We then return home and go about our lives as normal. Rarely do we ever actually take the time to stop and 'Think Through' the physiology and psychology of conflict. Neurologists go to school first. Ninety-five percent of their time is spent in books and lecture halls before they ever touch a human brain, let alone begin to cut into one. The kinesis of battle is useless if your brain hasn't been conditioned in the process of selecting the appropriate Tactical Response under the extreme stresses of Combat.

Taking the time to study Force Science and memorizing the scientific Laws of Combat will pay dividends tomorrow. Learning first what your body WILL do, will save you from spending tons of wasted time at the firearms range, inadvertently conditioning and encoding the 'Wrong' tactics for the wrong response.

Warning Apocalyptic Tsunami Ahead!!!

What's all the hype about? What's the big deal? You're ready you say? Oh yes, because you have a 1911 .45 ACP by your side at all times. You're ready for anything....

The truth? Physical confrontations with firearms is the most fluidly dynamic environment you will ever know. The overwhelming and unavoidable tidal wave of physiological and psychological effects, rates up there with an Apocalyptic Tsunami. Armed confrontations aren't action movies or video games and they're no 3 Gun match. There are no do-overs and EVERY error is immediately accompanied by a devastatingly lethal consequence.

Most armed citizens foolishly assume they're defensive firearms abilities are suffice. Many think that because they grew-up around firearms, carry one everywhere they go or because they're an expert 3 Gun competitor; they actually believe whole heartedly, they're ready for Combat. The problem lays in their ignorance of 'Fact' and of the unavoidable troubles which lurk ahead. They simply have no clue of the deluge that will wash over them like the worst kind of tidal wave imaginable. They aren't prepared for, or even aware of, the concept of 'Combat Gravity' nor are have the conditioned themselves to react appropriately in spite of the apocalyptic effects of Combat Stress.

For instance:

Action vs. Reaction:

1. The average untrained attacker can achieve a (90%) hit ratio on their prey, while the average untrained defender can only achieve upwards of around a (17-20%) hit ratio in response?

2. Statistics show that 90% of real-world shootings involve multiple rounds being fired and the average untrained person can shoot (4) rounds per-second. That's right, I said an "Untrained" person can shoot (4) rounds per-second.

3. Action is <u>ALWAYS</u> faster than reaction, it's a scientific fact. It takes the average human (0.30) seconds to simply react to a change in their environment. That's merely identifying the existence of 'Change', NOT reacting to said change. Now begins the daunting task of 'Reaction'. Given the overwhelming Stress Cocktail associated with any deadly attack, it takes a minimum of (0.53) more seconds to overcome and process the initial shock & awe of that attack. Then after all that; at (0.83) seconds, you can actually begin to implement some type of a physical response. Meaning, its not until (0.83) seconds into the fight that your brain tells your hand to move towards your holster.

4. Now consider the totality of the relationship between Action vs. Reaction, physics and your ability to survive the attack. The problem presented is a bad guy who's threatened or is actually using a gun against you. You're already drastically behind the Eight Ball. To survive you must identify the Threat, formulate a response, and then implement said response. As mentioned previously you're likely to sustain between (6.52 – 10.88) hits before you send your first round. If you don't believe this statistic, YouTube the 1981 President Reagan's Assassination Attempt. You'll see that John Hinckley Jr. was able to get (6) rounds off, before some of the Worlds most highly trained and capable individuals were able to finally subdue him.

5. This real-world Deadly Encounter is a perfect example because it gives you a snapshot of the cross-section of tactically minded persons present, from the horribly inept reporters and advisors and press sectaries to the elite of the elite Secret Service Presidential Detail members. It took each of these people so much time to respond that John Hinckley Jr. was able to shoot (6) times in (1.7) seconds, standing (10) feet away from President Reagan. His first shot was a headshot of all things. Four of his (6) shots hit multiple people including Regan all before he could be subdued. It's only certain Reagan would have been hit more would he not have had an entourage of people immediately present to protect his life. You can rest assure, you WON'T have a Secret Service Detail protecting you when you're attacked.

6. Remerging that bullets don't discriminate between right or wrong, friend or foe, victim or criminal, the reality is that molten hot, razor-sharp, metal objects will likely tare through your body at nearly 1,200 fps. This will cause profuse bleeding and immediately begin the ultimate shutdown of the majority of your overall bodily functions. It's only after this, that science shows that you're humanly capable to draw your weapon and begin the uphill battle of defending your life. Does that concern you? Does it make your stomach turn? It most certainly should. This is why the 'Right' kind of training makes all the difference beforehand.

Close Quarters Battles (C.Q.B.) / Proximity to Threat:

1. Distance equals time. The shorter the distance the less time one has to perceive an attack, react and then overcome the perceived deadly attack.

2. Distance also affects accuracy. Since you're reacting to attack, proximity is NOT your friend. The closer your Threat is, the less accurate he needs to be to achieve lethal hits. If your Threat is completely inept at 25 yards and couldn't even place one round on paper, at two or three feet, it's entirely possible that he'll score a possible and each of his rounds will rip through you before you even react.

3. At close proximity a number of other factors are immediately present. For instance, you can touch, feel, smell and even taste your Threat. The aroma of his body odor, the clamminess of his skin, the perplexing and paralyzing gaze of his lifeless thousand-yard stare. An up close and personal struggle for life with another human being is simply unmatched. It's daunting, spooky and emotionally unsettling even for the most experienced among us.

The Stress Cocktail:

1. **Fear (The Human Phobia of Death)**: The greatest most unavoidable innate reaction to a Deadly Threat is our natural fear of death. While some can learn to dilute and decrease the affect of this reaction, most people will be thrust into a whirlwind of paralyzing fear. Lt. Col. Dave Grossman coined it "The Human Phobia of Death." Like any of our most extreme phobias; spiders, snakes or heights, our entire being will immediately be galvanized. It will be like getting struck by lightning. Potent chemicals and hormones, like adrenalin and dopamine, will flood our bloodstream. The effects of which will throw your brain into an ultra DEFCON 1 level of security lockdown. From here, only the bodily functions required to perceive the Threat, determine an immediate response and then react to said Threat, will function. Everything else goes on lockdown. You simply revert back to the Caveman Brain where the only thing that matters is survival. It's at this moment that you will either Fight, Flee or Freeze. Sadly, most freeze, bringing unavoidable death.

2. **Heart Rate Explosion:** An adults normal resting heart rate lives anywhere between (60-80) bpm. Optimal competitive function lives between (115-145) bpm. At this range you're afforded the perfect combination of blood & oxygen flow throughout your body, which enables optimal performance of your entire

system. However, for the average citizen who's never faced an actual deadly attack, it's entirely possible for your heart rate to spike between (180-220) bpm or even higher. This is a very dangerous range. Even during normal everyday exercise, like running on a treadmill, if maintained over an extended period of time, this can easily cause cardiac arrest. This range is CATASTROPHIC while in heated battle. Due to the presence of the abnormally high levels of dangerous chemicals, the tidal wave of adrenalin and dopamine; which is violently pumping through you, if your heart rate isn't brought back to a safe level, cardiac arrest can occur within seconds as opposed to minutes. Even if you avoid cardiac arrest, at this range your body teeters between Conditions Gray & Black, meaning you're on the verge of total physical shutdown, like an engine seizing from a lack of oil.

3. **Loss of Peripheral Vision:** This is known as 'Focused Vision' or 'Tunnel Vision'. During attack the ONLY thing you will see is what you need to see. The color of the leaves on a distant tree, the little old lady crossing the street, or even the gigantic skyscraper standing directly behind the person trying to kill you. These are all irrelevant and will likely be completely erased from your perceived vision. This can be a good thing as it will give you a laser beam like, focused type of clarity of your Threat, but what if you're attacked by two or more individuals? Or what about when you consider your response and begin to fire back? Where are your rounds going to go should they miss? Will they hit the little old lady crossing the street? Or the family quietly eating their lunch in the restaurant directly behind your Threat?

4. **Loss of Near Vision:** Think about this, if you can't see your sights because your eyes simply can't see them; due to the fact that your eyes are ONLY trained on that which is trying to actively kill you, how are you going to use your sights to hit your Threat? While under attack, your eyes will see only what they need to see. Because your sights aren't trying to kill you, your eyes won't see them. Again, all your eyes car about is focusing on whomever or whatever it straying to kill you. This sort of phasing out of non-threatening objects is also true for other objects or non-treating people within the spectrum of your near vision.

5. **Loss of Depth Perception:** We rely on our ability to decipher depth in relation to our proximity to objects and surfaces around us. A drastic loss of this important sense would be like trying to fight while experiencing vertigo. Not knowing the true distance to objects in your immediate environment, increases the likelihood that you will trip or stumble, making you completely vulnerable and useless during attack. Understanding this now can help to elevate moments of panic should this occur during your fight.

6. **Auditory Exclusion:** As a result of the perceived likelihood of death, you may experience a temporary loss of hearing. Similar to 'Focused Vision', your ears will be trained on your Threat and will completely block out the plethora of sounds in your environment. A good example of this is best understood by those who've ever hunting before. When they raise their rifle and shoot their game, the report of the rifle sounds like a muffled pop-gun and their hearing is hardly affected. Yet shooting that same rifle on the range absent hearing

protection would leave their ears ringing in pain. Much of this is due to the high levels of adrenaline and dopamine that will surge through your body. In a real gunfight you'll likely experience the same kinds of auditory effects, where everything but your Threat appears muffled.

7. **Loss of Fine Motor Skills:** We rely on Fine Motor Skills for everything. In many ways it's what separates us from primates. Our ability to thread a needle provides the clothing on our backs. Our ability to put thought to paper, by holding a small pen to artistically communicate thoughts and ideas on paper, affords us the ability to expand our understanding. This fine motor skill alone; manipulating a pen to put thoughts on paper, provides blueprints of success for our children and our children's children. Our abilities to finely manipulate our bodies enables us to dominate our environment. However, while under deadly attack, your physiological system is taken out of balance and you will lose the ability to do simple physical things. Under these situations you're left with trying to force a square peg through a round hole or sinking a small nail on a wall with a 20 lb. sledgehammer.

8. **The Slow Motion Effect:** A well known phenomenon, which effects most people who experience extreme high levels of stress during deadly attack, is perceived slow motion. Time itself appears to literally come to a halt and barely ticks by. The best way to articulate this is to compare it to the scene in the movie 'The Matrix' where Neo dodges the torrent of bullets being fired at him, while he bends backwards and manipulates his body here and there, dodging every slow moving bullet slicing through the air. Similarly, time will appear to slow so much so that your movements may appear to be a sort of out-of-body experience.

9. **The Hyper Speed Effect:** Another phenomenon is the sense that your world has just jumped into a hyper speed wormhole. Sometimes people experience a weird mixture of the two where they experience a most bewildering tug-of-war of some outside force randomly pulling them from hyper speed to slow motion and back. A good example of this is seen in the movie 'Contact' when Dr. Ellie Arroway shoots through the Space Time Continuum and is violently torn from one world to the next. At one moment she sits in the harnessed seat of her spherical time machine. Then without warning, she's pulled up and out of the machine, looking down at herself from a God like third person view. For some people, a deadly attack can cause a very similar disturbing state of psychoses.

10. **Tormenting Thoughts:** Another extremely common effect from this type of stress is an onslaught of horribly vulgar and disturbing thoughts. For some they see their life literally pass before their eyes as if they were sitting in a movie theater; eating popcorn, while they quickly reach the climatic and tragic end of their life story. For others it's as crazy as the most exotic acid trip causing insane hallucinations. For instance, during one of my Deadly Force incidents, I swear I saw the suspect's vehicle turn into Magnetron, as it sped towards me, spilling sparks from its wheels which looked like waves of fire. A buddy of mine later explained to me that during one of his shootings, he saw a little green Leprechaun who continually taunted him throughout the

gunfight telling him, "You're gonna dieeee.... You're gonna dieeee..." These kinds of psychotic trips can make it extremely difficult to maintain effective situational awareness and decipher truth from fiction.

11. **Loss of Bowel & Bladder Control:** This is probably something you never thought of when considering how you'll respond to a deadly attack on your life. The reality is our bodies will react absent cognitive thought. At that moment there is only one goal in mind, survival. Average normal bodily functions will go on lockdown, providing ample energy and blood flow for those organs which are needed to provide the essential functions to secure survival. This means if you have a full bladder or are close to passing your last meal, it's entirely possible that you will do so right then and there.

Combat Hydraulics...

Hopefully this chapter underlined the fact that Combat is the most chaotically charged, out of control, consistently fast moving environment known to man. Its hydrostatic qualities are measured in thousandths of seconds multiplied by pounds per square inch. The fluidity of this environment is as volatile as the ocean tide and as random as the ebb and flow of its surge. Sure you might be a competent swimmer in the backyard pool. Hell, you may even be able to hold your breath under water for 5-minutes. Surviving the converging surge in the Straits of Magellan; where the Atlantic and Pacific meet, without a life vest or a wetsuit, that takes a level of proficiency I'd be willing to bet you don't have and Combat is easily as tumultuous as converging oceans.

The act of defending one's self with a firearm is a daunting task even for professionals. However, Combat can be tamed. You may have zero experience and have never actually been in a fight for your life before. You're Caveman Brain my even be pre-wired to Freeze. You may actually be the worst fighter in the entire universe, but don't lose hope. There are ways to pre-condition practical life saving responses and encode them deep within your brain's primitive DOS / C Prompt command. There are things you can do today so you can WIN tomorrow's battle and live to tell about it. It starts here, by preparing your mind for how your body WILL be affected. After this you can develop kinesthetic, Tactical Responses which can be performed in spite of these effects. It's only after you fully understand these scientific realities that you can begin to perfect your Kata and master your weapon.

While other training methods fall short, *ZuluFight* is founded on the very concept of Kata and is the most balanced approach capable of unthinkable levels of proficiency. It's movements have been painstakingly design to incorporate all aspects of firearms use. Through a zen-like attention to detail, the ZuluFighter is able to polish each and every aspect of firearms use, from the draw, it's presentation, manipulation, loading and reloading, malfunction mitigation, carry and shooting positions, from standing or even seated, standing idle and even moving as well as After Action Scanning techniques. There's nothing like it on the market, it's inexpensive, is performed when and where you'd like, requires no trips to the range and is the fastest way to achieve the highest level of firearms proficiency possible. It truly is a Firearms Total Training System.

3

To See Or Not To See...

"Don't concentrate on the finger..."
—Bruce Lee —

I remember a time when vehicles had the cool little things called Hood Ornaments. For those of you too young to know, Hood Ornaments were these interesting trophy looking things attached to the front hoods of most vehicles. They were similarly placed like a pirate ship's bow ornament. They stood about three or four inches off the hood and were typically shiny and chrome with the emblem of the vehicle's manufacture. I also remember them being quite popular, so popular that they became the cool thing to snap off and steal. In fact, there was a whole industry built around these quirky looking things.

What I don't remember is anyone attempting to use them as some sort of aiming reference. What I mean is, I was never taught nor can I ever remember anyone using their vehicle's Hood Ornament as a sort of 'Front Sight Post' like a handgun shooter would. When you drove a vehicle fashioned with a fancy dance ornament, you drove it the same way you would any other vehicle, you placed your hands at ten and three, looked down the road, put your foot on the gas and guided your vehicle to its destination using your eyes as the guide. Can you imagine attempting to maneuver your car down the road, at speeds well over 150 mph, while staring at nothing more than the front of the hood? I think we can all agree doing so would result in a crash and at those speeds the outcome is sure to be fatal.

There exists a major inaccurate and scientifically faulty technique being taught on nearly every firearms range around the world. To complicate matters, this grossly inaccurate technique is among the most controversial topics in firearms usage than any other. I'll refer to this controversy as 'Traditional Sighted Fire.' While it may have the appearance of logic on paper under normal everyday stress, Science tells us that while attempted under the stresses of Combat, Traditional Sighted Fire just doesn't work.

Ornaments Are For Looks...

Let's now explore the enigma of firearms sight use in close quarters engagement, specifically distances between zero and fifty yards. For purposes of ZuluFight, I'm focusing on the overall practicality of combative firearms use between these distances and its relationships with iron sight use. The vast majority of combat in general occurs within these ranges. Yes, there are plenty of examples, especially in military engagements, where you find intense battles beyond these distances, however this is very limited. The purpose of ZuluFight is to offer a better more practical tool which is tailor-made and practical for close engagements. The focus of this system is to provide you with a much more efficiently reliable and scientifically based approach to combative firearms use at these ranges, when the threat is up close and personal.

Now before I lose a large audience of readers, I want to make it evidently clear that the use of gun sights is a foundational building block for accuracy and for overall success with the implementation of firearms in general. The advantages in overall precision, gun sights provide cannot be argued. To become proficient with any firearm, one must learn to use it as though it were an extension of their body. However, to master it and obtain supreme accuracy, one must learn to exploit its sights and train their body to use its new "extension" like a surgeon and his scalpel.

One of the pillars of safe and accurate firearms use is drawn from one's ability to master their gun's sights. Yet there is a point at which one's ability to even use their gun sights is met with an obstacle larger than Mt. Everest. That point becomes evident during the combative application of fire under immediate and deadly attack. Nearly every firearms training system is founded on one's ability to apply foundational fundamentals while using their weapon, such as Traditional Sighted Fire, as a means to an end, resulting in the overall goal of sending accurate and focused fire on a particular threat. The problem arises when one of those fundamentals is absent or skipped.

Think of traditional firearms use as a three legged stool. One leg consists of Grip and Stance. The next is Sight Alignment and Sight Picture, while the third leg is Trigger Control and Follow-Through. Remove even one of these legs and your stool ceases to exist. Regardless of what some will say, out of these three legs, the most difficult and inherently prone to error involves the use of gun-sights. Most would say 'Trigger Manipulation' is much more elusive. However, let's use our control; (EM = T Squared), to measure these variances. When comparing Trigger Manipulation with Sight Use, we know that each require movement. With a trigger, you depress and squeeze the mechanism backwards towards you. With sights, you move the firearm and your eyes into 'Mechanical Alignment'. I would argue though that depressing a trigger mechanism that's mechanically designed to be easily manipulated and only operates in one unhindered direction, that this is much, much easier than bringing gun-sights into Mechanical Alignment. Now let's look at effort. Well it's obvious, if something is harder or requires more movement then it automatically requires more 'Effort'. But I would argue that it doesn't stop there. Brining gun-sights into Mechanical Alignment for just one shot requires an extraordinary amount of focus and eye strain. Repeating this with any consistency from shot-to-shot under low stress is even more inherently difficult. Achieving Mechanical Alignment during Combat while you're emptying your magazine? That my friends, is an impossibility. There are just way too many things going on at once for your human eyes to shift its focus from plane to plane with any consistency.

On the other hand, imagine the catastrophe of blind, unsighted fire, if your entire training system is based on the fundamentals of 'Sighted Fire'. What I mean is that if Force Science tells us that we won't see our sights because of our minds perception of an immediately present deadly threat, and our solution to that problem requires the use of gun-sights we can't see, then we've got ourselves a pretty significant problem. Sadly, most never take the time to consider this most life threating dilemma. You see if the crux of why you even train in the first place and all the effort you put into honing your precision is intended to give you the capability of defeating an actively attacking person who's attempting to kill you, and your response is based on your ability to acquire your gun-sights, then you really need to reconsider the 'Fight' protocol and quickly change that to one that has you 'Fleeing' with all your might. The reason is that once you find yourself thrust into a battle for your existence, you're going to find out that your entire training method, your tactics and your tool and all your dedicated efforts are completely impractical and ill suited for the occasion. You've essentially built a skyscraper on a mole hill and the mere presence of deadly confrontation; 'Combat', is an apocalyptic tsunami. You've dedicated an entire modus operandi to a technique that is destined for failure.

Sure, it's entirely possible to survive a gun battle through instinct alone. It's even possible to base your entire foundation on a system that won't work and still come out the victor. I mean even a blind squirrel finds a nut from time to time and a broken watch is right twice a day. However, it's a game of 'Chance', it's a gamble you can't afford to lose. The question is can someone be trained to use their gun-sights in a way that maximizes efficiency and practicality and can also be repeated during the deluge of Combat? The answer is an unequivocal yes and that's exactly what ZuluFight will do.

The fundamental difference between ZuluFight and Traditional Sighted Fire training and why ZuluFight is so superior during Combat, derives from the particular manner in which one uses their gun-sights in training. With Traditional Sighted Fire training, the gun-sights find the threat, with ZuluFight, the warrior finds his threat, locks onto said threat like a laser beam with their eyes, and presents their weapon while bringing their gun-sights into perfect alignment via Unconscious Competent Kinesis. The sights have been used a thousand times prior to the battle for the purpose of polishing and fine-tuning the 'Action' of drawing and presenting a perfectly aligned weapon without the need for Mechanical Alignment. This is achieved through focused attention to a carefully and strategically orchestrated, choreographed sequence of movements known as the 'Kata' of Firearms Self-Defense. Basically the ZuluFighter used their gun-sights a thousand times in simulated Combat and defeated their threat a thousand times before even meeting their threat. The ZuluFighter has trained to master their weapon and unconsciously use the weapon and its gun-sights with total competence, because their eyes have been trained to be the sights and their body the weapon. This is the essence of a Tactical Squared Response.

Traditional Sight Use...

There are many physiological reasons why Traditional Sighted Fire during close combat just won't translate. Sure we can see our sights in training and even under moderate levels of stress. However, seeing anything but your threat, while he's actively trying to kill you at close ranges, is virtually impossible. The overwhelming levels of stress experienced during mortal combat and the chemical effects this has on our physiology causes our bodies to respond and react in a manner very different to that which we're accustomed to in training. My quest was to find ways where sights could be used effectively because one can't ignore the superiority sight use has with overall accuracy. At the end of the day, it's only the hits that count. To understand this, we must first grasp the multiple components of firearms sight use in general. This is best summed up as Sight Alignment and Sight Picture.

Sight Alignment is the relationship between your firearm's front sight post and its rear sight. It also relates to one's perspective of their alignment. A wise man once told me "Equal light and equal height." The goal is to align your front post so it's level in height with your rear and there's equality of daylight on either side of the post, (i.1a and i.1b).

Traditional Sight Picture is similar. However, you're now aligning four independent objects; your perfectly aligned gun, with your thereat. Traditional Sight Picture consists of aligning your sights to the center mass of your threat, while simultaneously maintaining complete focal clarity of your front sight post, (i.2a). As you can see from this example, the rear sight and the threat are slightly out of focus.

Two problems arise with the introduction of combat stress loads. First, if your assumed focus and optimum clarity is on your post, yet your intention is to shoot your threat, then we have some problems. If your threat is not completely clear, then how do you know he's a threat and or how do you know he's still a threat? If our threat dictates our action, then isn't it only logical that we must maintain acute clarity of our threat?

Next, under combat situations our bodies do not have the ability to perform fine motor skills, multi-tasking goes out the window and one's ability to mentally transition between multiple focal planes, while maintaining consistent clarity of tiny objects, is hopeless. As learned in Chapter 2, when someone is attacked and when that attack is immediate and up close, our bodies are designed to first identify the threat to our very existence and second to react. This is as innate a response as breathing. The attempt to defy this physiological function is as logical as someone trying to hold their breath to death, it just can't be done.

Our bodies are designed to function and function they do. Bodily function has nothing to do with cognition but everything to do with our ability to operate with inherent automation, independent active thought. Because of this it's virtually impossible to intentionally and truly hold one's breathe indefinitely. Our bodies are designed to live and to live they must breath. The physiological consequence to such a lack of oxygen is hypoxia. Basically at the point of hypoxia, you'll simply pass-out. Your Caveman Brain overrides the stubborn Intelligent Brain, which is telling you to hold your breath. It simply knocks you out and it's off to counting sheep for a minute. While you lay there; now unconscious, your primitive, innate breathing function returns, charging your blood system with oxygen and the lights soon come back on.

Trying to see anything but your threat during an up-close gun battle? Yeah not so much... Our Caveman Brain kicks in, visually locks down on our threat like a laser guided missile while quickly determining a response. Sometimes this response works and we survive to tell the story. However, often times our Caveman Brain provides us with a square peg for a round hole. My goal was to find a way to train my Caveman Brain to select the perfect solution for an imperfect problem.

Using The Right Tool...

The dynamics of Combat are vast. My intent isn't to dissect it into its many molecules. I only wish to express the divergence it has with range related shooting and quite frankly 99 % of the firearms training methods in use, while also providing a solution to this problem. Too many of us for far too long have been sold a lie. It's about time we put aside our opinions and let science sort it out. As I've stated previously, the topic and debate on Traditional Sighted Fire vs. Point Shooting, focusing on your threat while shooting, is hot with emotion and theory. I'm not so concerned about peoples 'feelings' and 'opinions' when it relates to the topic of Combat. At the end of the day a particular tactic or method either works or it doesn't. In terms of the best methods and tactics when it relates to Combat, they must all be founded on the Keep It Simple Stupid (KISS) theorem. Murphy's concept that "If it can go wrong, it will go wrong" is true and always picks the worst times to ring true. The more complicated your response, the more prone it is to fail and gun-sight use couldn't be any more complicated than it already is.

I want to make it very, very clear yet again, I believe iron sights play an important role in firearms use and I'm not advocating the abstinence of their use. However, the role of iron sights in Combat is a most limited one, requiring a bit more understanding through the exploration of the physics of Combat. In Combat, a well-trained Point Shooter has the best chance of not only hitting the threat, but more importantly, winning the battle. Historically, the best close quarters battle (CQB) shooters, have always been Point Shooters, i.e. Wyatt Earp or Billy The Kid types. These guys used inferior weapons and ammunition without sights and could, at the drop of a hat, draw and accurately fire their weapons from their hips, unsighted, with rapid succession at extended ranges. Yet the Sniper in me knows the greatest possible accuracy is achieved only through the proper use of Sighted Fire. So this tug-of-war battle of techniques is as close to a stalemate as one could possibly find.

Holographic & Reflex Type Sights...

Before we go further though, I must also touch on the topic of holographic type gun sights. This would include the wide range of sighting systems such as EOTech, Aimpoint, Red-Dots and others like the Leupold DeltaPoint Reflex. They work and they work damn well! These types of sighting systems are a much more practical means of aiming than traditional iron sights. Why, all you have to do is overlay an image on your Threat and follow through with good trigger squeeze. As long as the sighting system is zeroed, you're shooting within the prescribed distance the system was sighted for, and you're using sound shooting fundamentals, you're going to hit with accuracy.

These systems save the shooter tons of time and allow for extremely quick sight acquisition from shot to shot. They're also crazily easy to use. I've seen upwards of a ninety -percent increase in accuracy by simply giving someone a weapon equipped with such a device and telling them to put the dot on the target and shoot. They're just too practical and effective to overlook. However, they are an accessory that one can't rely on. When they work, they're great but if for some reason yours goes down or the battery is depleted, you're back to square one.

The very same stressors affect the practical use of holographic and reflex type sights during Combat as do effect a shooter who's attempting to use Traditional Sighted Fire. However holographic sights are so simplistic in their application, that it is entirely possible to train one's self to see the holograph while engaged in combat. This does take a TON of practice under high stress. It's also very dependent upon the actual amount of stress overload one experiences during their particular gun-fight. So you may just notice that while engaged in one particular battle, you're able to utilize the sight, while in another one, you might not notice its even there. It really boils down to 'Stress Inoculation Training' where you're exposed to extreme degrees of stress during training while being required to perform very difficult Combat related tasks so as to inoculate you much like a flu shot does.

Needless to say, there is a scientifically supported place for these types of sighting systems in combat. ZuluFight is intended for close encounters within fifty yards. Since only circumstance dictates the distances at which we fight, it would be a very wise idea to equip yourself with a means of fighting past this range. Let's take for instance an Active Shooter incident in an office building with a commons area or hallway, seventy-five yards or longer in distance, or maybe a parking lot. Being able to seamlessly transition to a sighting system tailored for battle, pays dividends. Amalgamating ZuluFight with a holographic or reflex type sight would be the best of both worlds. Find one that works for your intended applications.

The Front Sight Method...

Now what about the Front Sight Method? This is where the shooter ignores the rea sight notches and focuses on the Front Sight or 'Post', then goes about overlaying or 'Indexing' the crystal clear Post on a blurry target. I'll admit, this is a VERY effective method and can make quick shots and target transitioning and extremely easy task. Why, because its MUCH more scientifically sound than Traditional Sight Use. With the Front Sight Method, the shooter focuses on ONE thing, the Front Post, which is completely consistent with the KISS approach. However, science is clear, during an actual fight for your life, your ONLY going to see one thing..... your Threat. In turn the Front Post will prove to be as elusive as a cheetah on the savanna. You're just not going to be able to transition your eyes off your Threat, ignore your Threat who's trying to kill you, focus your attention on your Front Post who's not trying to kill you, and index that Post on an actively attacking Threat who's most likely shooting at you by now. It's just NOT going to happen.

To a Front Sight shooter though, this divergence isn't necessarily doom and gloom. A Front Sight shooter develops the habit of 'Indexing'. Due to the simplicity of this method and its relationship to the Threat and how close a Front Sight

Method's Sight Picture is with a real-world Combat Sight Picture, the Front Sight shooter develops a much more practical process of shooting. Over time, the habit of 'Indexing' becomes so basic that they don't even cognitively need to search for or even focus on their Front Post, it just happens. Because of this, during a real fight; when their eyes are focused on the Threat, the Front Sight shooter can quite simply 'Index' a blurry Front Post over a crystal clear Threat and send accurate fire their way.

So what if we expanded this theory further? What if we landed on a training method which better aligns the 'Shooter' to their Threat while their gun follows? Wouldn't it make sense to train your eyes to 'See' what their going to see rather than wasting effort training your eyes to see something they won't see tomorrow?

A New Way To See...

A Piñata is a sure ingredient to some good laughs, a few screams and a mad dash for yummy candy at any party. But remember how impossibly hard it was to find those damn things while blind-folded, let alone hit it with confidence and consistency? What about how tiring and frustrating it was, all while being the focus of everyone's taunting?

Do you look at our finger when extending your arm to push a door bell or do you look at the door bell? When you drive your 3000-pound bullet down the road, do you stare at the steering wheel while you maneuver through traffic? Or do you focus on the vastly changing environment around you while you kinesthetically guide your projectile to its final destination? When you're at Home Plate and you're awaiting the delivery of a 90 mph fastball, do you stare at the sweet spot of your bat with anticipation of sending a fly-ball over the center field bleachers? Or do you focus on the incoming ball?

Using your gun sights in close combat with the intent of hitting your threat is not only an attempt to defy physics, but it's like trying to hit a baseball you can't see. You couldn't hit a 3-foot by 3-foot slowly moving Piñata dangling above your head as a kid, with any amount of consistency, so what makes you think you could hit a 2.5-inch ball moving at 90 mph, with your eyes closed?

There is another perspective which offers the best of both worlds, Contemporary Sighted Fire through Procedural Memory or Kinesthetic Combat Shooting, i.e. ZuluFight. I want to make it precisely clear again, I said 'Sighted Fire Through Procedural Memory'. This technique combines Traditional Sighted Fire and Kinesthetic Procedural Memory techniques for a more contemporary Tactical Squared Response. The result is the Unconsciously Competent use of gun sights for a Point Shooting style immediate threat-focused response. It's the most natural and practical technique around. It's actually been in use for thousands of years in all other forms of combat to include Ancient Martial Arts.

Science tells us it's physiologically impossible for humans to acutely see two independent objects located in two completely different focal planes at the same time, with any hope for equality of clarity. Simply put, our ocular system is wired so that our brain uses both eyes collectively to isolate and identify a particular object amongst a plethora of other colors and shapes in the same environment. This means, our eyes can't operate independently and see both what's to our left and to our right at the same time; nor can we see a small 1-inch rear sight 24 inches in front of us, line up a ¼ inch high post located another 3 inches forward, while also clearly identifying and seeing an attacker even 5 feet in front of you, all at the same time with equal clarity.

The truth is firearms training systems, which encourage Traditional Sighted Fire in combat, are founded on the ignorance of well intentioned individuals with a warped understanding of the physiological parameters of combat. I say parameters for good reason. While it's possible to overcome particular deficiencies which come to the surface during combat, there are a number of very true realities that restrict overall bodily function while actively engaged in combat. Just as the Laws of Physics and Gravity prevent even the most earnest attempts to walk on water, the Laws of Combat have their own unavoidable limitations on exactly how we respond to deadly threats.

Forgive me ahead of time for the blunt rant that follows. I mean no disrespect to anyone who shares an opposing viewpoint. When it comes to such an important topic as combat and one's ability to achieve superiority over their adversary, I don't have much time for political correctness. This isn't a debate over who makes a better truck, Ford or Chevy? Nor is this a deliberation between the exceptional qualities of flavor of vanilla ice-cream vs. chocolate. As a trainer, what I'm addressing is more than opinion, it's about the tools I introduce to my students and the methods in which I train them to use those tools, where the outcome could either save someone's life or cost someone their dad, brother, mother or sister.

This is a topic of life so I'll be blunt and say this; those individuals who hold to the opinion of Traditional Sighted Firer during combat have been brought up sipping on the same glass from Mr. Kool-Aid man himself, believing a myth that's as factual as the Tooth Fairy. The choices are clear. You could try Jedi mind tricks like Obi One Kenobi. You could attempt to catch flies with chopsticks while blind folded like Mr. Miyagi. Or you can choose a training method with a scientifically proven approach, guaranteed to give you a fighting chance. My advice... Stop drinking the Kool-Aid and switch to ZuluFight, it tastes better. Here's why...

Fact vs. Fiction...

As discussed previously, science teaches us that as stress levels increase our body's fine motor functions rapidly decrease. When faced with the overwhelming Apocalyptic Tsunami accompanied with Deadly Encounters, our entire physiology succumbs to its all consuming power. As a result, our brain's experience a complete polar shift. Due to such a sudden and abrupt about-face, our entire body's normal body functions go on ultra lockdown. Expecting to accomplish complicated, time consuming and finely tuned physical tasks; with ANY degree of competence, under such a state of being, is as farfetched as taking a giant leap off a skyscraper and expecting wings to suddenly sprout from your sides.

Besides the loss of fine motor skills, we also experience and acute affect to our hearing, time awareness and heart rate among other things. Most notably, our entire visual function is drastically diminished. Many people associate the later with 'Tunnel Vision' or 'Focused Vision'. Furthermore, studies have shown that when placed in such a state of motor shutdown, our field of peripheral vision is nearly equal to that of closing one eye while looking through a toilet paper tube with the other.

Traditional Sighted Fire requires Conscious Competence, the most complicated kind of physiological function and completely cognitive-based. While reacting to a lethally attacking threat, it's simply physiological impossible to perform such a task. If I can't sprout wings and fly, walk on water or see through walls, then how can I for a moment expect my eyes to see something they're completely and utterly unable to see in a fight? Over the past few decades, a number of highly trainers within the Special Operations Community have dabbled in the theory of Sighted Fire Through Procedural Memory. What they've found is that it just makes more sense. As apposed to attempting to defy physics, they've developed similar training systems aimed at helping the elite of the elite in honing and perfecting their craft. Many well respected SOF Units have already adopted these practices and are transitioning to a more contemporary use of sights in training for a much more bulletproof solution tomorrow when those rounds count.

Hood Ornaments had their purpose but today they've been replaced for a much for streamlined approach. Similarly, ZuluFight is your streamlined approach to a more practical use of gun-sights.

Bruce Lee once said "It's like a finger pointing away to the moon. Don't concentrate on the finger or you will miss all the heavenly glory."

He also said, "You must be shapeless, formless, like water. When you pour water in a cup, it becomes the cup. When you pour water in a bottle, it becomes the bottle. When you pour water in a teapot, it becomes the teapot. Water can drip and it can crash. Become like water my friend."

You see like 'Water' its essential the warrior becomes the 'Sights' in battle. God gave you two eyes to 'See', your gun can't see a thing, it was made to be pointed and then fired. During a gunfight there is but one overriding focus, your 'Threat'. In the heat of combat, your 'Threat' represents the most celestial Super Moon of all. Focusing on anything but your 'Treat' will cause you to miss it completely and missing your 'Threat' is a bet you'll only lose once. Become the sights and win the fight.

4

Training For Mastery

"Bad practice makes poor habits and poor habits are the fastest way of getting killed in Combat."
—Instructor Zulu—

To achieve mastery, the warrior knows ahead of time what to expect tomorrow. The warrior has already studied and fully grasps the dynamics of conflict so that when he trains he trains with a propose. The warrior trains with laser-focused concentration to hone and perfect each and every minute movement. The warrior perfects his Kata to assure its structural integrity as well has insuring that each and every movement is performed slowly and with active cognition so that the breath of his action is completely cohesive with its intent which is to kill his enemy before his enemy kills him. The warrior fights his battle a thousand times over before ever meeting his adversary. The warrior utilizes his gun-sights as confirmation to assure the presentation of his weapon was performed with utmost precision like a surgeon and his scalpel. The warrior perfects his craft by mastering his weapon, its functions, components and even its malfunctions. The warrior trains and trains and trains until his weapon becomes an extension. Only then is the warrior ready.

The intent of this chapter is to provide tactile definition to this Total Training System to afford you the ability to perform it with perfection. It's vital that you pay attention to detail and study this section in its entirety prior to jumping ahead to the exercises. There are a number of important concepts you'll need to fully understand in order to perform ZuluFight like a master. Taking the time to read through these instructions now will save you precious training time tomorrow.

ZuluFight is by far the only stand-alone system which provides true Firearms Mastery. This is because the system utilizes every aspect of firearms use. What makes this system so special is the fact that it's a Firearms Total Training System. Not only will it provide the warrior the ability to employ immediate and accurate fire, it also enables the warrior a surefire means of mastering all other aspects of firearms use to also include reloads, malfunctions and manipulation. But it doesn't stop there; it's just as affective while training with a Long Gun like a rifle or shotgun as it is with a handgun. It still doesn't stop there. Another amazing outcome is the warrior's ability to become proficient with their holster, sling and shooting positions. This is great for the average citizen and will provide a method of training that gives them much more for less. This is huge for law enforcement and other tactical professionals especially when acquiring new holsters, sling systems, magazine pouches or platforms. Mastery of things like holsters can be had in a matter of two complete ZuluFight sessions.

You'll even find this system to be an extremely good physical workout, similar to a trip to the gym. Because of the repetitive nature of the system and the fact that the warrior will spend much of their time in a crouched position while extending and raising their arms many times, this system can be thought of as a sort of Tactical Yoga. After your first session, you'll experience the very same soreness and muscle fatigue you'd expect after a good workout using free weights. Repeated and regular use of the system will keep your muscles toned, fit, flexible and strong. Complete the advanced movement drills and you're sure to stay in shape.

Equipment Needs...

You'll be surprised to find, ZuluFight requires very little equipment with zero cost-reoccurrence. The ability to train from your home with what you already have is unparalleled. For the most part you need an operable firearm. My suggestion is a semi-auto pistol as these provide the best all-around practicality for combative situations. Remember (KISS) while selecting your firearm. The less amount of buttons, safeties, catches and parts, the less inherent the firearm is to malfunction or failure. On a similar note, your ability to multi-task goes out the window during times of Combat. So expecting to press this button and pull that catch to release this safety, is a pipe dream when bullets start zinging past you or even worst, right through you.

For best results and for the highest degree of overall firearms proficiency, I suggest investing in a few invaluable items:

1. Situational Awareness is an essential part of a sound defense. After Action Training is among the most overlooked aspects of Firearms Self-Defense training. Conditioning yourself; beforehand, to be stay aware tomorrow takes a special type of training. ABCs Tactical Training Aides (ABCs) are an ingenious way to perfect your After Action Scan. They train your eyes to actively 'Seek' directly following your defensive response or during tactical lulls. ABCs are extremely inexpensive and extraordinarily easy to use. Best of all they can be used for both Dry & Live-Fire Training. ABCs will take your Situational Awareness to an unthinkable level. Find yours today at zulutactical.com/ABCs

2. Another thing to consider are 'Snap-caps' or 'Dummy Rounds'. These are very inexpensive tools and can be found at most any gun shop. Some firearms actually require Snap-Caps for Dry-Fire Training, so make sure to consult your owner's manual to learn more about the requirements of your specific firearm. My favorites are 'Saf-T-Trainer Dummy Rounds'. I've also had great success with 'A-Zoom Snap-Caps'. Regardless of where you find them, they are truly invaluable. Snap-Caps are also extremely helpful during Malfunction Training Drills. They're great visual Aides to help visually indicate a particular type of

simulated malfunction. Snap-Caps are also greatly helpful in the overall use of a semi-auto firearm for Dry-Fire Training due to the fact that they will allow for proper charging of your weapon for simulated fire. It's highly recommended you purchase enough Snap-Caps to fill three magazines. They can also be purchased in bulk and come in almost every caliber.

3. Extra firearms magazines are a huge plus. This isn't mandatory but for many reasons, an extra magazine can go a long way especially for firearms combative situations. Extra mags will also be beneficial when practicing reloads and malfunctions. For average citizens, three extra mags should be plenty. If you're a concealed carry person, I suggest carrying a spare mag with you at all times. Also, having extra mags allows you to cycle your mags to lengthen the overall lifespan of your mags. If you're a professional the more mags the merrier. I carried three extras on-duty and also had a hasty vest containing another four handgun mags and ten rifle mags. This may appear overboard to you, but I prepared for a sustained battle not duel at town square. The reality of a heated gun battle with a planed and experienced foe means you could easily expend hundreds of rounds in a few minutes. Should a Mumbai style terror attack or an Active Shooter incident occur on my watch, I was ready for anything. Magazine carriers are also important. If you're an armed citizen there are some great options for both belt carry and inside the pocket carry. Professionals also have a plethora of options.

4. A decent holster is a great all around safe and practical means of training and carry. If you're an armed civilian or professional, there's a plethora of decent duty and concealed carry options available to you. If you don't have a holster or prefer not to get one, don't worry. You can still perform the vast majority of exercises, just skip the holster section.

5. A quality Par-Timer is an invaluable addition to your training kit. These ingenious gizmos are a great way to test the efficiency of your Kata. In fact, there are whole portions of ZuluFight dedicated to Par-Time training at the end of both the Handgun and Long Gun sections. Like Snap-Caps, Par-Timers can be found at most gun shops or online. I suggest one that offers both random and timed beeps.

6. Lastly it's important to consider what you'll be wearing or carrying in a real-world deadly encounter. If you're a police officer or tactical professional, it's imperative that you train with the gear you're likely to be using day in and day out. There's a lot to be said about using the same equipment in training that you bring to the fight tomorrow. This really is a hugely important concept to grasp. Remember to dress for success. Wear the type of clothing you'd most likely dress in on a daily basis. Don't train in your undies if you don't plan on fighting in them. If you're a concealed weapons carrier or armed citizen, pay special attention to how you perform the holster exercises. Use the holster or set-up you're most likely to use any given day. Remember the goal is to

repeat perfect movements from each position as if you were actually in a fight for your life.

Planning For Success...

Now that you have your gear situated, sit down and plan out when you'll be performing your Kata. For instance, determine what day of the week and what time of day would be best suited. Each section of exercises i.e. Handgun SUL Ready Position or Handgun Type 2 Malfunction, takes approximately 45-minutes to complete. Set this time aside and don't skip it. Most of us know going to church for an hour each week won't get us to Heaven. However, failing to practice the Kata of Firearms Self-Defense just may get you there tomorrow. This is among the most important types training you'll ever perform. The hope is that you'll never need these skills but if you do, ZuluFight is your best chance for survival.

Mindset...

As mentioned previously, the whole purpose of your training and the intent behind your Kata is for one thing and one thing only, to 'Kill' your threat before they 'Kill' you. It's not about 'Wounding' or simply 'Shooting' your threat, it's about the act of 'Killing.' Failing to grasp this all important concept will expose your psyche and make you vulnerable to Combat Paralyses when real bullets are zinging past your ears. On that note its vital to maintain this mindset when you approach your training session, as you perform your training and following your training. Your training for competition and it's not a game. Your efforts are to hone and polish your craft to make it the best possible fighting solution for tomorrow. So take things serious.

While you're performing your Kata and upon the decision to draw and present your weapon, it's important to cognitively think "FIGHT! FIGHT! FIGHT!" This is huge because while encoding the kinesthetic movements of your fight, you're also etching; deep within your psyche, the image of an actual person attempting to kill you. While thinking "FIGHT! FIGHT! FIGHT!" its important to also think that the person; in this case the Threat Target, is actually trying to kill you. The idea is to try your best to simulate the cognition of your life in limbo and you making the cognitive decision to defend it. The combination of these two Procedural Memory functions, both physical and psychological will ensure that tomorrow's response has density and weight.

Similarly, you'll notice that after each 'Fight' portion of a given exercise, you'll be asked to "Assess" your situation. It's really important to understand the importance for this transition of thought. Make sure to pause for the prescribed time and actually think "Assess... Assess... Assess..." What this does is psychologically separates the 'Fight' from the 'Assess' phase of your response. It's vital to learn how to properly assess your situation to remain situational aware of everything that's going on around you. In training you'll utilize this time to confirming your gun-sights are in proper Mechanical Alignment to assure your movements were performed with perfection. It also encodes the process of 'Seek' protocol for after your fight

Remember that Force Science shows us that during times of Combat stress, it's likely that you'll experience 'Tunnel' or 'Focused Vision'. Telling your brain to "Assess" in training and completing your 'After Action Scan' will encode a habit of seeking for other threats and cause your focus to broaden while you regain normal vision. Just as importantly, the process of cognitively thinking 'Assess' will actually disassociate the 'Fight' portion of your Kata. This way you're not training yourself to attempt to find your gun-sights after each round is fired, during a real-world engagement. Skipping these steps will actually negate your training all together.

Perfecting Your Kata...

Above all else the number one most important objective is to perform each exercise with utmost perfection. This is why slowing each movement down to a sloth's breath is important. The concept of 'Slow is smooth and smooth is fast' rings true here. The slower you perform your Kata, the more cognitive focus you can direct towards each particular and individual movement within a sequence. Failing to do so will inevitably cause you to encode poor habits. Again, your number one goal is to perform perfect movements and repeat each movement perfectly twenty-five times perfectly prior to moving on to the next section.

It's important to understand your initial movements won't be up to par, but that's the whole reason for training. As you 'slowly' perform your Kata, make sure to self-coach. You are your best coach; self-coaching will allow you to quickly identify training errors before they become habit. Focus on each movement and analyze its quality. If you notice you're doing something wrong, determine how to correct it and correct it. To accomplish perfect movement, you must focus on extremely 'slow' and deliberate movements while cognitively thinking through each movement. The running theme if you haven't picked up on it, is the word 'slow', the only way to truly hone your movements are by performing them slowly. Refer to the image guide at the back of this book as much as needed. This provides a quick reference on how to perform particular movements and proper techniques.

The other underline theme here is to 'think'. Don't forget the important information you learn in chapter 2 pertaining to the brain. It's vital to actively think while moving. ZuluFight engages multiple muscle groups causing them to act together for one harmoniously choreographed action. The just is that you're training to focus on your threat who's actively trying to kill you, present a perfectly aligned weapon without the need to manually align your gun-sights, and finally end your fight through the simulation of a perfect trigger squeeze. The greatest muscle in your body is your brain; it's your brain that will help achieve the highest degree of perfection. Cognitively thinking through each particular movement while training today, will give your body the highest degree of Procedural Memory Encoding for a perfect fighting solution tomorrow. Again its vital to think about how your muscles feel while manipulating each movement especially once you've achieved perfect alignment. Knowing how your muscles 'feel' while your weapon's sights are in perfect Mechanical Alignment will allow your body to subconsciously feel its way to perfect alignment when all you can see is the person who's trying to kill you tomorrow. Memorize these feelings to better identify accuracy of moment. Pay attention to detail and assure each movement is perfect. Quality of movement is your goal, not speed. Save the speed for Par-Time drills.

Threat Identification & Focus...

The next important step is to ground yourself in the concept of 'Threat Focused Training' which is key to the correct performance of ZuluFight. This concept goes hand-and-hand with 'Sight Use' which we will discuss later.

It is highly suggested you always train using a life size picture of an actual criminal's face as a target. Either remove yours from the back of this book or download another Threat Target by visiting our website at www.zulutactical.com/downloads and select it from the ZuluFight section. For best results, have your Threat Target laminated. From there simply scotch tape it to the wall of your choice. Training with actual images depicting human faces during both Live or Dry-Fire Training, is most unsettling. Our society has taught us that this is taboo and wrong. It's also an eerie and uncomfortable experience in and of its self. This is precisely why you should train exclusively with human face targets. Inoculation and desensitization of your psyche is just as important to inoculation yourself to the other Laws of Combat discussed in Chapter 2.

Remember the 'Intent' of your Kata is in the preparation of defending your life against future attack from vicious criminals, so you can 'Kill' them before they kill you. Staring into the eyes of an actual killer thousands upon thousands of times in training, will desensitize your psyche and inoculate you from the intimidating facial expression your future threat is likely to display. It will also eliminate the natural apprehension of 'Killing' that you were born with. Again, the business of training to 'Kill' in Self-Defenses is much more than shooting paper. Killing another human is a disgusting reality that completely contradicts all of our foundational 'Western' morals and values. Yet, it is a reality that must be accepted, overcome and performed with the highest proficiency should that unfortunate skill-set be called upon.

Likewise, focusing on your threat throughout the entirety of the engagement is extremely critical and is an imperative skill-set to hone. Chapter 2 should have underlined and highlighted just how chaotic a real-world deadly encounter truly his. The multiple comparisons between Combat and the power of the oceans, specifically the hydraulic principles of their surge, should not be overlooked or taken lightly. Combat is truly the most fluidly dynamic environment known to man. The reality is that when you are confronted, it will be by one; or more, actively aggressive constantly moving individuals who are surrounded by a just as constantly moving environment. This being said, it is essential that you master the concept of 'Threat Focus'. You must maintain the highest clarity of your threat(s) at ALL times throughout the encounter, no matter how stressful or distracting the environment.

Training yourself to identify your threat is also paramount. If you can't see your threat, you can't beat your threat and your threat ends up being an offal lot like that elusive 'Piñata' discussed earlier in Chapter 3. The concept of 'Threat

Identification' is an extremely important subject and will greatly affect the outcome of your fight. Just as important as identifying your threat, it's important to know who's actually a threat and who's not. When bullets start flying, the last thing you wanna do is turn around and blast granny by accident when the guy who's shooting at you is actually standing next to her. This is why 'Situational Awareness' goes hand-in-hand with 'Threat Identification'.

For the most part your threat is likely to be within arm's reach, however there are times when you could be attacked from across a room or even across a parking lot. There are also external factors such as low light, fog or even bright light; which floods out your visual clarity of the threat. All these greatly diminish your ability to see your threat. For these reasons it's compulsory to develop the ability to correctly identify a threat.

The most tactically effective Threat Identification Technique was developed by the United States Special Forces. This five step process; when practiced, will assure you appropriately scan your environment the right way.

DELTA Threat ID:

1. **Whole Body**: The first step is to cognitively thinking about 'Who' you're actually looking at. Is it a man or woman, adult or child? Who are they? Are they in a uniform? Do they have a badge? Could they actually be a friend? These are all very important questions one must train their minds to 'Think' while their eyes 'Seek'. Seeing a person's 'Whole Body' will help elevate the chances of you mistaking a friend for a foe.

2. **Hands:** Your next step is to find their 'Hands'. It's been said "It's the hands that kill." Finding someone's hands will aid in determining if the possible threat is armed or not. Are they armed with a weapon or holding a cell phone? Seeing a weapon does NOT mean to 'Shoot' or that they're a threat. They could actually be assisting you or a police officer. This is why all five steps are important.

3. **Waistband:** Now it's time to check their waistband. If you didn't see a weapon in their hand, it doesn't mean they're not hiding one on their waist or in their waistband. Visual check their waist. What are they wearing, could something be hidden there? These are questions you should be asking.

4. **Arm Span:** After this you need to check their immediate surroundings. Is there anything in there 'Reach' which could be used as a weapon? This will also give you the ability to identify other persons and or other potential hazards.

5. **Demeanor:** Lastly, you need to check their face and body language. This is the most overlooked step and usually be the key to uncovering the truth. Remember 90% of communication is 'Non-Verbal' meaning body language often times says all. You should be asking yourself if they appear happy, sad or even angry? Look into their eyes, are they letting off that they're hiding something or being tricky? Or does their

demeanor tell you they're an innocent bystander or an armed citizen attempting to aid in your defense?

Each of these steps are extremely important in assuring that you correctly identify a threat. Remember the most overlooked step is 'Demeanor'. You need to confirm that they actually 'Look' like a threat, either through their facials or body language. Becoming proficient in this technique requires practice. It's most easily achieved during Stress Inoculation training like Force on Force Training simulations. However, an easy way start building solid Threat Identification habits, is by actively identifying random people on a daily basis. Follow the SOF Threat ID process as you interact with other people on a daily basis. Ask yourself if the random person approaching you is a 'Threat'? then follow the five easy steps. Doing this on a regular basis will cause your mind to develop a habit of always scanning your environment for possible threats and will keep you situationally aware at all times.

Sight Use...

One of the biggest differences between ZuluFight and other firearms training methods relates to the relationship between maintaining a 'Threat Focused' mindset; as mentioned previously, combined with a completely unique way of actually using your gun-sights. With other training methods, the warrior attempts to use their gun-sights to find the threat, wasting an enormous amount of time while also setting you up for failure during a real-world deadly encounter. With ZuluFight the warrior uses their eyes to 'Seek' and 'Lock On' the threat and uses their gun-sights for training to 'confirm' or 'measure' the quality or accuracy of the presentation of their weapon. This saves a ton of time which you simply can't afford to waste. This also assures you maintain effective Situational Awareness throughout the fight.

What this means is with ZuluFight, you use your gun-sights 'After' you depress the trigger, much like a long jumper uses a tape measure to measure the quality of his jump, 'After' he jumps. While this concept may appear ass backwards, there is a scientific basis for this technique. As was discussed in Chapter 2, Force Science makes it crystal clear, seeing anything but your threat during a real-world deadly encounter at close range is virtually impossible. So training to do something wrong is the wrong way to train. Your gun-sights should only be used to confirm quality of the kinesthetic movements of the draw and that your trigger squeeze was performed in unison and with perfection. Each combination of perfect movements is forever etched deep within your Caveman Brain, for a pre-programmed, precision aimed, shooting solution for tomorrow's battle.

So with ZuluFight the key is to focus on your threat and simulate shooting your threat by depressing the trigger with a perfect trigger squeeze, all the while maintaining visual clarity of the threat. Sight Picture; what the shooter sees in relation to their gun-sights and the threat, is of particular importance while performing the exercises. ZuluFight Sight Picture is vastly different than Traditional Sight Picture. With Traditional Sight Picture, the gun-sights are in focus while the threat is somewhat out of focus and fuzzy. However, with ZuluFight the threat is always in perfect focus, while you maintain a 'Fuzzy' peripheral awareness of your weapon in front of you.

To better understand this, perform the following task:

1. Stand 5 feet away from a wall of your choice.
2. While facing the wall, focus on a particular portion of the wall, i.e. a picture frame or spot.
3. Extend your arm and point at that picture or spot while maintaining visual focus on the picture or spot.
4. You should clearly see the picture or and barely notice your outstretched pointed finger, which appears 'Fuzzy'.
5. Now slowly transition your focus to your outstretched finger and back to the picture. This is where your bullet would strike using a ZuluFight Sight Picture.

Traditional Sight Use requires a person to first, identify the threat as a threat, then transition focus from the threat; which is actively trying to kill you, to now pick-up and track your Front Post while presenting their weapon and pointing it at the threat; who's already moved from where you they were first seen, then perfectly align the tiny Front Post with the almost as miniature Rear Sight, then attempt to overlay those sights on the threat by moving them in unison, while maintaining perfect Manual Alignment and then finally squeeze the trigger, all within an extremely limited par-time window and all while being shot or shot at. Sounds simple right!?!?!

Now consider how 'Simple' and 'Logical' the ZuluFight method is. First the warrior identifies their threat. Next they visually lock down on their threat using their eyes like a sort of laser aiming devise. Now while maintaining perfect focus of their threat, they present a perfectly aligned firearm and depress a perfect trigger squeeze. Basically the ZuluFighter sees their threat and shoots their threat. Now ask yourself which method makes more sense?

Like a long jumper who jumps first then measures, the ZuluFighter, fights first in training then measures the accuracy of their movements. They move first, presents a perfectly aligned weapon, depresses the trigger; ever so smoothly, then they measure sum of that movement based on the resulting position of their gun-sights. If the gun=sights aren't perfectly aligned, the warrior brings them into Mechanical Alignment. Next the warrior cognitively thinking about how that particular position of Mechanical Alignment actually feels. They focus their minds on the feeling of each particular muscle group; specifically, in his chest and upper body, to memorize the way perfect Mechanical Alignment 'Feels' in training. It's this relationship between efficient movement during training, how that movement feels, and the overall clarity of the cognition of that movement, which enables them to present a perfectly aligned firearm every time.

Remember, you won't see your sights in Combat. Training to do the right thing is the right way to train. One thing you must keep in mind is that ZuluFight trains the warrior how to align their sights through kinesis. In order to achieve perfect kinesis, you MUST use your gun-sights. However, it's 'how' you use them that makes the difference. So always remember to transition back to your gun-sights 'After' you complete your simulated fight to measure the accuracy so you can make the appropriate adjustments to avoid encoding poor kinesis.

Spot Checks...

Quality of movement means everything. One way to double check your progression is to randomly perform a 'Spot Check'. This is where you randomly audit how well you're doing. To do this:

1. Acquire your Tactical Stance (i.16)
2. Focus intently on your Threat Target
3. Assume your desired Start Position i.e. SUL Ready Position (i.20a, i.20b & i.20c)
4. Close your eyes while intently focusing your thought towards where you last saw the threat
5. Think "FIGHT! FIGHT! FIGHT!" as you raise and present your firearm and fully depress the trigger for a simulated fire once reaching Natural Arm Extension.
6. Open your eyes to confirm your gun-sights are in proper Mechanical Alignment exactly where you intended to hit the threat.
7. If they're dead on, you're progressing well. If you're off, you need to correct this. Don't cheat yourself, be honest. If your gun-sights aren't exactly where you intended to shoot your target, you MUST hone this position better
8. To fix this, bring your gun-sights into Mechanical Alignment (i.1a & i.1b)
9. No cognitively thinking about how your muscles feel; specifically, your chest and upper body, while in perfect Mechanical Alignment (i.1a & i.1b)
10. Memorize this 'Feeling' of Mechanical Alignment (i.1a & i.1b)

Initially you may notice your gun-sights are completely off the entire Threat Target. This is completely normal and will get better as long as you're paying attention to the quality of your movements and correctly using your gun-sights to confirm the accuracy of your movements while you train. Performing regular 'Spot Checks' will quickly tell you exactly how you're doing and protect form as a safeguard in assuring you're not inadvertently encoding poor fighting habits.

Fighting Stance...

How you stand and posture yourself in training is an integral ingredient to encoding the most Tactically Squared Response tomorrow. We touched on this earlier in Chapter 2. Studies clearly show you will resort to a crouched position during an attack. This can be easily likened to that of a basketball player playing defense or a shortstop who's crouched and ready for wherever the next ball goes. The example of the 1981 President Reagan Assassination Attempt and how people physically reacted directly following the first shots; specifically, their stance, is but one example. Think back over your life to a time when you were startled by an extremely loud 'Bang!' when you least expected it. I'd wager to say you assumed the very same position that everyone else on Earth does when they first realize they may be under attack.

I call this position your Natural Transition Stance. This stance is as inherently innate a response as our body's automated breath functions. It happens without thought and is immediate. In fact, it can be likened to any other response function. Remember that 'Knee Jerk' test the doctor gives you during exams when they lightly tap your knee with the miniature triangular, rubber tipped mallet? Remember how your leg magically jumps without you actually telling it to? Now think about all those times you saw your doctor tap your knee, knowing exactly what was going to occur and trying to control the 'jerk' and prevent it from happening. You can't, no matter how hard you try, as long as your nervous system is working properly, your leg will jerk regardless of your efforts to stop it. The very same is true about our body's natural Transition Stance immediately following the notion that we may be under impending attack.

I call it the Natural Transition Stance because it's a position our body falls back to during the Polar Shift of our brain function while it goes from our Intelligent Brain to our Caveman Brain. Have you ever seen a computer system crash, sending it to a 'Blue Screen' where all you see is a matrix of coded lines with random alpha numerics quickly processing across the screen? That's exactly what the Natural Transition Stance is, it's your body's 'Blue Screen'. Once there, your body naturally pauses while your brain reverts back to the archaic DOS or C Prompt function where all you have is computer code. From this Natural Transition Stance, your body can immediate employ your Caveman Brain's solution based on the particular 'Top Secret' fold your Amygdala retrieves. You will either Fight, Fight or Freeze and the Natural Transition Stance sets your body up for the perfect place to make this response from, a crouched coiled and ready to spring stance.

Standing flat footed while performing ZuluFight will only work against you during a real-world fight for your life. Due to how similar your Natural Transition Stance is to the Modified Isosceles Stance, I strongly urge you to ONLY practice from this Fight Stance. If you happen to be a Traditional Isosceles or Traditional Weaver style person, switch! Remember "If you wanna be rich do what rich people do" and likewise "If you shoot like the best train like the best." Don't waste your time training yourself to try and defy the Laws of Physics and Combat because you can't. Doing so will only increase your response time. That means your threat could easily fire 11 or more shots before your actually able to initiate your response.

The Modified Isosceles position will also most closely resemble a Natural Fighting Stance which is identical to that of your Natural Transition Stance. The Modified Isosceles provides the most practical mobility as well as the best overall base, especially when considering the degree of recoil absorption obtained during rapid fire situations. Keep in mind, standing in a crouched position for any length of time is difficult but training for a battle isn't intended to be an easy one. This is why you're encouraged to take multiple breaks throughout each session, to enable you to maintain perfect form every time.

About that trigger...

Now here's where attention to detail and commitment to perfection makes all the difference. If you allow yourself to be sloppy with trigger manipulations, you'll essentially sabotage the entire system. Remember, with this system you use your gun-sights 'After' the trigger squeeze as a method of measuring accuracy. So if you slap, yank or jerk your trigger, you'll have no way of knowing where your gun-sights were when you depressed the trigger or if they were in Mechanical Alignment. In turn you'll likely encode poor Procedural Memory fight habits.

It's been said that Trigger Manipulation translates to ninety-percent of an individual's ability or inability to shoot accurately. While I agree that trigger manipulation is a huge ingredient to success, what it really boils down to is mastering the Kata of Firearms Self-Defense. Its about slowing everything down to allow for 'Perfect' movement. Every aspect of ZuluFight is performed with a commitment to perfection, so must mastering the trigger is huge. The perfect trigger squeeze can be summed up by saying it's a careful degree of the economy of effort balanced by the economy of movement one uses while squeezing the trigger rearward.

Simply pulling the trigger means you're likely to yank it. Doing so will cause you to miss especially while shooting multiple rounds. The objective is to squeeze your trigger all the way to the rear with consistent and uninterrupted travel at an appropriate speed for the appropriate need. It's like driving a car around a corner. If you attempt to input too many RPMs while driving around a tight, slick corner, the risk is running off the road. The same is true for trigger manipulation. Learn to harness the RPMs. Harnessing speed of travel will translate to effective and proficient trigger discipline. Over time you'll learn to increase RPMs around tight corners through the efficiency of your overall ability to control the movement of your weapon while squeezing the trigger to the rear.

Important ZuluFight Terms...

There are a handful of frequent terms which you'll see throughout your ZuluFight training. It's extremely important that you fully understand what these terms mean prior to attempting the training. The following will better define these terms:

1. **Finger Outside Trigger Guard (F.O.T.G.):** Firearms 'Safeties' are an oxymoron. They were created for idiots and are far from safe. The only safety is your brain's control over your Trigger Finger. For this reason, one of the pillars to Firearms Safety pertains to how and when you use your Trigger Finger. Throughout ZuluFight training, you'll notice the acronym "F.O.T.G." refers to you remembering to keep your Trigger Finger outside the Trigger Guard and completely off the trigger until its time to practice a simulated fire. An example of just how to make sure you're encoding sound "F.O.T.G." habits is by reviewing the applicable images at the back of the book. (i.3)

2. **Natural Arm Extension:** There is a place at which your arms naturally extend and rest while holding a handgun in front of you. One

of the most effective ways to master the kinesis of shooting is by harnessing your body's natural ergonomics. As Bruce Lee put it, "Don't fight the water, be the water." Similarly, its wise to train yourself to incorporate your body's natural ergonomics into your fighting solution. That being said, you should develop an 'Ergonomic' way to extend your handgun in front of you. Find that 'Natural' position where the extended firearm feels comfortable allowing your Support Hand to pull backwards against your Gun Hand creating a vice like grip.

3. **Natural Cradle Rest:** Your body also has a natural position of ergonomics when it relates to how you hold a Long Gun. Due to the overall length and weight of a long-gun, this natural position of ergonomics is slightly different than your Natural Arm Extension. In fact, is more like a closer 'Cradling' position, hence the name. With practice you will find that perfect spot where your long-gun naturally rests in the cradle of your arms, where it becomes much easier to hold and manipulate over long periods of time. This is your Natural Cradle Rest where your long-gun 'Rests' while you use it.

4. **Manual Alignment:** Another term you will see a ton of is the concept of 'Manual Alignment'. This is the exact position of where your gun-sights are in perfect alignment with each other, your eyes and the threat. This is the position you'll use to measure the quality of your movements. It's also the exact firing position you will attempt to memorize physically so you can 'Feel' your way to perfect alignment without having to search for your gun-sights.

5. **Simulated Fire Mode:** ZuluFight is a simulated Dry-Fire Training system. That means you do NOT use live ammunition at anytime during the training. Instead you 'Simulate' Live-Fire through the use of Snap-Caps and 'Dry' fire your weapon. The concept of brining your weapon to the Simulated Fire-Mode means that through the use of Snap-Caps, you load your weapon making sure it's chamber has a 'Simulation Snap-Cap' inside and the weapon's slide or action is fully closed and ready for Simulation Fire. Again there is absolutely NO live ammunition used for ZuluFight Dry-Fire training.

6. **Following Through:** After performing a simulated fire, you will be instructed to pause for a (2) count while "Following Through" what this means is to keep your trigger finger on the trigger and pressed rearward for the entire time of the (2) count. This is an important skill-set to encode. Follow Through insures you don't move your firearm directly following your trigger squeeze and prior to the bullet exiting your handgun. The slightest movement of your weapon while the bullet travels through your barrel will inhibit your overall accuracy down range.

7. **Stepping Off Line:** Another important habit which should be so well engrained in your response during a deadly encounter, is your ability make yourself a more difficult target. Stepping out of the way does two things. First is obvious, it makes you harder to attack. Secondly, it causes your Threat to react and track your movement while you

perform an assessment of your situation, clear your malfunction or reload etc. This should be completed after each simulated fight so it becomes muscle memory during a real-world incident.

8. **After Action Scan:** As mentioned previously, Situational Awareness is an essential part of a sound defense. For many, many reasons you need to know what's going on around you during the gun-fight. You may be attacked by multiple threats from different locations. There will likely be innocent bystanders randomly walking about in your immediate surroundings. Your backdrop; or what lays beyond the threat, is also extremely important to know so you don't end up inadvertently shooting someone else. Finding places of cover and concealment as well as avenues of escape are also extremely important. After Action Scans are how you train your eyes and brain to work together to 'Seek' these things out.

    You will be instructed to perform an After Action Scan following each use of Simulated Fire. It's crucial that you steer away from simply making this a habitual turn of the head. Instead, you need to specifically encode the 'Act' of 'Seeking'. This means that while performing your After Action Scans during training, you MUST actively seek and identify random objects in your immediate surroundings. We've made this easy for you through the use of our ABCs Tactical Training Aides (ABCs). They truly are the BEST way to perfect your After Action Scan both on and off the firearms range.

9. **Discarding Magazines:** During Reload and Malfunction drills you may be asked to "Discard" your magazine. This means exactly what it says, get rid of it and get rid of it quick. The intent of this training is to train for battle. If your weapon goes empty during a fight for your life, the empty or fouled, that magazine is useless. Wasting time to retrieve and stow it is just wasting time. Likewise, in training, you must get in the habit of tossing your empty or fouled magazine to the ground to allow yourself quick access to the mag-well for recharging. If you're concerned about damaging your floor or magazine while tossing it to the ground, place a thick rug below your training area or conduct your training in a carpeted area.

10. **The 'Slid Sweep':** Throughout ZuluFight you'll be instructed to acquire common positions or perform redundant actions. For instance, while performing reloads, you'll do this from the 'Reload Ready Position' or prior to your After Action Scan, you'll assume the 'C.Q.B. Ready Position'. The intent is to encode a particular degree of redundant efficiencies from one discipline to another regardless of what discipline you complete. This way no matter what movement you're performing, you can seamlessly transition to a completely different one. Along this thought process, I approach the 'Racking' of a slide for purposes of loading, a little different than others. Since it's inevitable that malfunctions will occur at some point, I trained myself to 'Sweep' the Ejection Port of my weapon each time I move my hand back to grab the Slide. The movement of a 'Slide Sweep' for malfunctions is identical to moving your hand to the rear to grab the back of your Slide for loading.

So by infusing the 'Sweep' to each time you Rack your Slide, you in turn make the 'Sweep' an automated response anytime you attempt to manipulate the Slide. Another huge benefit is that by doing this you preemptively develop a 'Fix' for those times when your weapon Stovepipes without your knowledge and all you're doing is reloading. The 'Sweep' in this circumstance would immediately clear the Stovepipe saving tons of time if you had to reverse your thought after finding out that your reload wasn't working.

11. **(2) Count Pause:** Throughout your training you will be instructed to "Pause for (2) count" This is an extremely important step and is strategically placed at critical points within the overall sequence of your response. During a real-world engagement, the hardest function to perform are transitions of thought and movement due to an increase in required cognitive processing. 'Thinking' during high stress is a very, very difficult task. Taking the time to 'Think' at very crucial transitions is huge. The objective is to pause and allow yourself to 'Think' specifically about what your next move will be so you initiate it with perfection. Using a cognitively based Conscious Competent approach at these critical junctures during training will encode a seamless Unconsciously Competent automated transition tomorrow. Don't be lazy with your 'Pause', think through them and utilize this time to make sure your transition is initiated with a well planed approach.

12. **Continuous Movement Drills:** At the end of each section i.e. C.Q.B. Ready Position or Holstered, you'll notice a that you'll be asked to perform the main 'Movement' portions of that discipline while continually taking small steps. The intent is to infuse movement in your defense. You may assume that randomly walking in small circles doesn't appear to be that difficult. More seasoned shooters may also assume such simplistic movement training isn't as tactically sexy as the more advanced movement drills performed on some firearms ranges. Well your assumptions would be wrong. Any amount of movement even random tiny circles or even walking back and forth makes your job harder and that's the intent of these drills. Performing a 'Perfect' trigger squeeze or even presenting your weapon with kinesthetic alignment is difficult enough without moving let alone trying to clear a malfunction while constantly walking around and around. The intent of these drills are to cause your mind and body to work harder while maintaining 'Perfect' Kata. Start out slow in the begin. Then as time goes on and you progress through the honing of your Kata, up the tempo of your movement drills.

13. **Par-Time Drills:** There are two types of Par-Time Drills performed during ZuluFight training. The first is the 'Random Beep'. This is where you set your Par-Timer to make a randomly timed audible beep. Upon hearing the beep, you draw and perform a simulated fire as quickly and smoothly as possible. The second are 'Decreasing Par-Time Seeped Drills'. This means set your Par-Timer to perform two tasks. First to give you a 'Random Beep' which indicates when to draw and second to

perform a 'Stop Beep' which tells you when you should have finished the simulated fire. Incrementally decreasing your part-time window is a great way to better polish your Kata since it adds a fair bit of peruse.

The Master...

Firearms mastery is only accomplished through a commitment of gaining extreme proficiency in ALL aspects of firearms use by dedicating one's self to a prescheduled and religiously followed training regimen. Mastery comes from the perfection of one's Kata. Procedural Memory Encoding is true for quality training as well as inferior training methods. Bad practice makes poor habits and poor habits are the fastest way of getting killed in Combat.

Incorporating both a solid understanding of Force Science combined with a dedication to the 'Kata' of Firearms Self-Defense, will give you the surest solution for tomorrow's deadly battle. ZuluFight allows you to train like an Aikido Master. It provides you the platform to use laser focused, Zen like Consciously Competent thought to allow for the best overall Procedural Memory Encoding. It slows things down giving you the opportunity to practice 'Firearms Free Throws' so you can master the kinesis of shooting at the same time you train your psyche to consciously 'Kill' your threat a thousand times before you actually meet them.

Other Dry-Fire Training methods fall short, focusing on but a few ingredients to a solid fight. ZuluFight is your healthier more balanced option; it's your 'Firearms Total Training System' that conditions the body and the mind for both the fight that lays ahead and the pure mastery of your firearm, its components, accessories, operation and even malfunctions. ZuluFight allows you to master all this today, so you can fight and win tomorrow.

Final thoughts...

The ZuluFight training guide gives a step-by-step cook book formatted guide on how to master the Kata of Firearms Self-Defense. Particular instructions are given relating to the manipulation of individual components of a given firearm. This is intended to be a 'guide'. If the movement instructs you to engage or disengage safeties and your weapon doesn't have one, ignore that particular task and move to the next. Victory of tomorrow's deadly encounter is won first at home. ZuluFight is the key to your quest for firearms mastery. Train with dedication, consistency and the expectation of perfection.

FORCE SCIENCE INSTITUTE ® found at Forcesicence.org and KILLOLOGY RESEARCH GROUP found at Killology.com, should be your starting points. They both offer a treasure trove of information. They even have books and training opportunities, which you should take full advantage of. Knowing the parameters of how your body WILL respond beforehand, will insure you're not wasting your time developing useless tactics. The pre-study of Force Science will insure you condition your Caveman to win the day by pre-conditioning it to develop practical and effective fighting habits ahead of time. Discover the truth you won't learn on the firearms range.

Are you aware of the legal storm you'll face should you be forced to use Deadly Force to protect your life or someone else's? Simply being 'Justified' won't protect you from extremely costly Civil Lawsuits. Regardless of the outcome, your actions will be scrutinized on both the Criminal and Civil levels. Your innocence is completely depended upon how well you prepare for this unavoidable legal battle and how well you articulate your actions. ZuluTactical has you covered. Go to Page 206 and learn why ZuluShield is Firearms Legal Defense made easy. Discover how you can protect against future legal action today, learn the secrets behind a bulletproof Firearms Legal Defense. Believe me, you simply can't afford to overlook this most important task.

Take your training to the next level. Use the QR Code on Page 207 or visit our website to learn about our amazing training opportunities. We offer civilian, private and professional firearms training as well as tactical training from basic to advanced, regardless of your skill level. For the most reliable, effective and practical firearms self-defense, check out our Handgun and Rifle pipelines. If you're looking for more advanced opportunities, check out our Advanced Tactics and ZuluWarrior pipelines. We even have a myriad of other cool training opportunities like Active Shooter Response, Tactical Home Defense and more.

The Evolution of Tactical is here. We also specialize in training opportunities which are exclusively offered to ladies. Learn more about ZuluGirl today by using the QR Code on Page 207. It's hands down the best firearms training opportunity for ladies of all backgrounds and skill levels. No more worrying about arrogant and chauvinistic guys. Approach your next training with confidence, peace of mind and go away with an unmatched level of satisfaction and capability.

Join our team. Use the QR Code on Page 207 to follow us on Facebook and stay up to date about all things *ZULU*, join TeamZulu today. To hear the latest about important topics about Self-Defense, Firearms, Tactics, Products and much more, check-out our ZuluTalk blog. Lastly tell 3 friends and 3 family members, tell those you care about. Educate them about the best way they can be prepared; should they ever need to defend their lives, is with ZuluFight today. Train Today So You're Ready Tomorrow!

ZULUFIGHT

- Fight To Win System -

Instructions

ZuluFight Safety Rules:

ZuluFight is a Dry-Fire firearms training simulation system. This means there is **ABSOLUTELY NO AMMUNITION** permitted or even used while performing its exercises. Furthermore, there is **ABSOLUTELY NO AMMUNITION** permitted in the training area at **ANY** time whatsoever while performing said training.

1. ZuluFight is divided into two disciplines, Handguns and Long Guns i.e. Rifle & Shotguns, with a number of exercises from different 'Ready Positions' i.e. SUL Ready, Holstered and more, as well as the ability to complete multiple drills to include Par-Time speed drills, malfunctions and reloading.

2. Designate a routine & private training area. This location should be free from distractions, secluded and hidden from public view.

3. Carefully designate your backstop. If at all possible, choose a wall which offers the best overall bullet stopping capabilities. (just in case)

4. Start by pasting the ZuluFight Threat Target on your preselected backstop. Scotch Tape works great! Remove your Threat Target from the back of this book or download & print a copy at *www.zulutactical.com/downloads* and select it from the ZuluFight section. It's also highly suggested you have your Threat Target laminated. This will exponentially lengthen its durability and lifespan.

5. Again there is ABSOLUTELY NO AMMUNITION!!! Always insure your firearm and ALL its magazines are COMPLETELY UNLOADED and there is NO AMMUNITION in the training area WHATSOEVER.

6. Take appropriate care and caution while unloading your firearm. Assure that you maintain safe muzzle discipline. Also make sure your fingers are kept outside the trigger-guard and off the trigger while unloading.

7. Triple check to assure your firearm and ALL of its magazines are COMPLETELY UNLOADED and free from any and ALL firearms ammunition.

8. It's highly suggested you place your loose ammunition in a Ziploc bag while training. This keeps your loose rounds in one place, prevents the possibility of a loose round remaining in the training area and protects them against misplacement and or damage.

9. After you have assured that your firearm and its magazines are empty and free from ALL ammunition, take your Ziploc bag of loose ammunition and place it in another room to prevent the possibility of a Negligent Discharges and or other mishaps.

10. Snap Caps or Dummy Rounds are highly recommended and may actually be required per your firearms owner's manual for Dry-Firing training. Be sure to acquire enough for your training needs and use them every time you perform ZuluFight.

11. Select a training spot approximately 5-7 yards away from your now posted Threat Target. This is the exact spot in the training area or room where you will complete your ZuluFight session.

12. Next, select your discipline, i.e. Handgun or Long Gun.

13. Now select your exercise, i.e. SUL Ready, CQB-Ready or maybe a drill.

14. Follow the step-by-step guide through the entirety of each specific exercise.

15. located at the back of your printed book are a number of quick-reference images to show how to properly perform particular ZuluFight techniques. Don't be shy, view these as much as you require so you maintain perfect form every time.

16. Unless attempting Par-Time Drills, make sure to repeat each exercise slow and deliberately, while cognitively thinking through each individual movement. This maximizes Procedural Memory Encoding via Kinesthetic Repetitive Conditioning.

17. Maintain the same Tactical Stance as well as the exact same amount of grip tension through the entirety of your ZuluFight training. This will greatly assist in maintaining consistent natural sight alignment as well as encode perfect firearms kinesis.

18. Take breaks frequently to help with muscle fatigued. Repeat the exact same perfect movements (25) times prior to moving to the next movement. Muscle fatigue induces poor movement and repeating poor movement encodes poor fighting habits. Remember (*EM = T Squared*) master the efficiency of your movements.

19. Par-Time Drills are specifically designed as a means to test one's overall proficiency. If you miss your threat, being the fastest gun in the West is as useless as a paper-bottomed boat in rough seas. Maintain proper form as speed increases. It's critical to master each movement with the intent of shaving milliseconds off your overall response time for a completely Tactical Squared Response.

HANDGUN

ABSOLUTELY NO AMMUNITION!!!

C.Q.B. Ready

Movement 1 (C.Q.B. Ready)

1. Assure weapon is in Simulated Fire Mode.
2. Perform the following sequences while maintaining complete focus on the Threat and using peripheral vision if needed for the following functions.
3. Acquire your Tactical Stance. (i.16)
4. Pause for (2) count.
5. Cognitively think "FIGHT! FIGHT! FIGHT!" while focusing on the Threat.
6. Acquire a C.Q.B. Ready Position w/F.O.T.G. (i.19a, i.19b & i.3)
7. Inhale slowly and deeply, while slowly extending arms to Natural Arm Extension, while also acquiring proper grip-tension, disengaging the safety mechanism, keep your weapon level, bringing it up to eye-level, while pointing it at the Threat while keeping the Threat in focus. DO NOT DEPRESS TRIGGER (i.7a, i.7b & i.2b)
8. Pause for (2) count.
9. Cognitively think "Assess...Assess...Assess..."
10. Confirm proper Mechanical Alignment (i.1a) If not in Mechanical Alignment, bring weapon into Mechanical Alignment, while cognitively thinking about how your arms and chest feel once in Mechanical Alignment.
11. Memorize the feeling of Mechanical Alignment.
12. Step offline either left or right.
13. Exhale slowly, while relaxing your grip-tension and slowly return to a C.Q.B. Ready Position w/F.O.T.G. (i.19a, i.19b & i.3)
14. Perform an After Action Scan, checking to your right and behind, your left and behind. Visually and cognitively identify a specific object in the process i.e. ABCs Training Aides (i.26a, i.26b, i.26c & i.26d)
15. Pause for (2) count.
16. Repeat sequences 1-15 (25) times.

Movement 2 (C.Q.B. Ready)

1. Assure weapon is in Simulated Fire Mode.
2. Perform the following sequences while maintaining complete focus on the Threat and using peripheral vision if needed for the following functions.
3. Acquire your Tactical Stance. (i.16)

4. Pause for (2) count.

5. Cognitively think "FIGHT! FIGHT! FIGHT!" while focusing on the Threat.

6. Acquire a C.Q.B. Ready Position w/F.O.T.G. (i.19a, i.19b & i.3)

7. Inhale slowly and deeply, while slowly extending arms to Natural Arm Extension, while also acquiring proper grip-tension, disengaging the safety mechanism, placing your trigger finger on the trigger, keep your weapon level, bringing it up to eye-level, while pointing it at the Threat while keeping the Threat in focus. DO NOT DEPRESS TRIGGER (i.7a, i.7b & i.2b)

8. Pause for (2) count.

9. Cognitively think "Assess...Assess...Assess..."

10. Confirm proper Mechanical Alignment (i.1a) If not in Mechanical Alignment, bring weapon into Mechanical Alignment, while cognitively thinking about how your arms and chest feel once in Mechanical Alignment.

11. Memorize the feeling of Mechanical Alignment.

12. Step offline either left or right.

13. Exhale slowly, while relaxing your grip-tension and slowly return to a C.Q.B. Ready Position w/F.O.T.G. (i.19a, i.19b & i.3)

14. Perform an After Action Scan, checking to your right and behind, your left and behind. Visually and cognitively identify a specific object in the process i.e. ABCs Training Aides (i.26a, i.26b, i.26c & i.26d)

15. Pause for (2) count.

16. Re-engage the safety mechanism.

17. Pause for (2) count.

18. Repeat sequences 1-17 (25) times.

Movement 3 (C.Q.B. Ready)

1. Assure weapon is in Simulated Fire Mode.

2. Perform the following sequences while maintaining complete focus on the Threat and using peripheral vision if needed for the following functions.

3. Acquire your Tactical Stance. (i.16)

4. Pause for (2) count.

5. Cognitively think "FIGHT! FIGHT! FIGHT!" while focusing on the Threat.

6. Acquire a C.Q.B. Ready Position w/F.O.T.G. (i.19a, i.19b & i.3)

7. Inhale slowly and deeply, while slowly extending arms to Natural Arm Extension, while also acquiring proper grip-tension, disengaging the safety mechanism, placing your trigger finger on the trigger, keep your

weapon level, bringing it up to eye-level, while pointing it at the Threat while keeping the Threat in focus and depressing trigger all the way for a simulated fire upon reaching Natural Arm Extension (i.7a, i.7b & i.2b)

8. Pause for (2) while following through.
9. Cognitively think "Assess...Assess...Assess..."
10. Confirm proper Mechanical Alignment (i.1a) If not in Mechanical Alignment, bring weapon into Mechanical Alignment, while cognitively thinking about how your arms and chest feel once in Mechanical Alignment.
11. Memorize the feeling of Mechanical Alignment.
12. Step offline either left or right.
13. Exhale slowly, while relaxing your grip-tension and slowly return to a C.Q.B. Ready Position w/F.O.T.G. (i.19a, i.19b & i.3)
14. Perform an After Action Scan, checking to your right and behind, your left and behind. Visually and cognitively identify a specific object in the process i.e. ABCs (i.26a, i.26b, i.26c & i.26d)
15. Pause for (2) count.
16. Rack weapon slide to return to Simulated Fire Mode.
17. Re-engage the safety mechanism.
18. Pause for (2) count.
19. Repeat sequences 1-18 (25) times.

Movement 4 (C.Q.B. Ready)

1. Continually take small steps forward, backward left and right while repeating all sequences of Movements 1-3 (25) times.
2. Repeat all sequences of Movements 1-3 (25) times using a Par-Time Random Beep to initiate simulated fight.
3. Continually take small steps forward, backward left and right while repeating all sequences of Movements 1-3 (25) times using a Par-Time Random Beep to initiate simulated fight.

SUL Ready

Movement 1 (SUL Ready)

1. Assure weapon is in Simulated Fire Mode.
2. Perform the following sequences while maintaining complete focus on the Threat and using peripheral vision if needed for the following functions.
3. Acquire your Tactical Stance. (i.16)
4. Pause for (2) count.
5. Cognitively think "FIGHT! FIGHT! FIGHT!" while focusing on the Threat.
6. Acquire a SUL Ready Position w/F.O.T.G. (i.20a, i.20b, i.20c & i.3)
7. Inhale slowly and deeply, while slowly extending arms to Natural Arm Extension, while also acquiring proper grip-tension, disengaging the safety mechanism, keep your weapon level, bringing it up to eye-level, while pointing it at the Threat while keeping the Threat in focus. DO NOT DEPRESS TRIGGER (i.7a, i.7b & i.2b)
8. Pause for (2) count.
9. Cognitively think "Assess...Assess...Assess..."
10. Confirm proper Mechanical Alignment (i.1a) If not in Mechanical Alignment, bring weapon into Mechanical Alignment, while cognitively thinking about how your arms and chest feel once in Mechanical Alignment.
11. Memorize the feeling of Mechanical Alignment.
12. Step offline either left or right.
13. Exhale slowly, while relaxing your grip-tension and slowly return to a SUL Ready Position w/F.O.T.G. (i.20a, i.20b, i.20c & i.3)
14. Perform an After Action Scan, checking to your right and behind, your left and behind. Visually and cognitively identify a specific object in the process i.e. ABCs Training Aides (i.26a, i.26b, i.26c & i.26d)
15. Pause for (2) count.
16. Repeat sequences 1-15 (25) times.

Movement 2 (SUL Ready)

1. Assure weapon is in Simulated Fire Mode.
2. Perform the following sequences while maintaining complete focus on the Threat and using peripheral vision if needed for the following functions.
3. Acquire your Tactical Stance. (i.16)

4. Pause for (2) count.
5. Cognitively think "FIGHT! FIGHT! FIGHT!" while focusing on the Threat.
6. Acquire a SUL Ready Position w/F.O.T.G. (i.20a, i.20b, i.20c & i.3)
7. Inhale slowly and deeply, while slowly extending arms to Natural Arm Extension, while also acquiring proper grip-tension, disengaging the safety mechanism, placing your trigger finger on the trigger, keep your weapon level, bringing it up to eye-level, while pointing it at the Threat while keeping the Threat in focus. DO NOT DEPRESS TRIGGER (i.7a, i.7b & i.2b)
8. Pause for (2) count.
9. Cognitively think "Assess…Assess…Assess…"
10. Confirm proper Mechanical Alignment (i.1a) If not in Mechanical Alignment, bring weapon into Mechanical Alignment, while cognitively thinking about how your arms and chest feel once in Mechanical Alignment.
11. Memorize the feeling of Mechanical Alignment.
12. Step offline either left or right.
13. Exhale slowly, while relaxing your grip-tension and slowly return to a SUL Ready Position w/F.O.T.G. (i.20a, i.20b, i.20c & i.3)
14. Perform an After Action Scan, checking to your right and behind, your left and behind. Visually and cognitively identify a specific object in the process i.e. ABCs Training Aides (i.26a, i.26b, i.26c & i.26d)
15. Pause for (2) count.
16. Re-engage the safety mechanism.
17. Pause for (2) count.
18. Repeat sequences 1-17 (25) times.

Movement 3 (SUL Ready)

1. Assure weapon is in Simulated Fire Mode.
2. Perform the following sequences while maintaining complete focus on the Threat and using peripheral vision if needed for the following functions.
3. Acquire your Tactical Stance. (i.16)
4. Pause for (2) count.
5. Cognitively think "FIGHT! FIGHT! FIGHT!" while focusing on the Threat.
6. Acquire a C.Q.B. Ready Position w/F.O.T.G. (i.20a, i.20b, i.20c & i.3)
7. Inhale slowly and deeply, while slowly extending arms to Natural Arm Extension, while also acquiring proper grip-tension, disengaging the safety mechanism, placing your trigger finger on the trigger, keep your

weapon level, bringing it up to eye-level, while pointing it at the Threat while keeping the Threat in focus and depressing trigger all the way for a simulated fire upon reaching Natural Arm Extension (i.7a, i.7b & i.2b)

8. Pause for (2) while following through.
9. Cognitively think "Assess...Assess...Assess..."
10. Confirm proper Mechanical Alignment (i.1a) If not in Mechanical Alignment, bring weapon into Mechanical Alignment, while cognitively thinking about how your arms and chest feel once in Mechanical Alignment.
11. Memorize the feeling of Mechanical Alignment.
12. Step offline either left or right.
13. Exhale slowly, while relaxing your grip-tension and slowly return to a SUL Ready Position w/F.O.T.G. (i.20a, i.20b, i.20c & i.3)
14. Perform an After Action Scan, checking to your right and behind, your left and behind. Visually and cognitively identify a specific object in the process i.e. ABCs Training Aides (i.26a, i.26b, i.26c & i.26d)
15. Pause for (2) count.
16. Rack weapon slide to return to Simulated Fire Mode.
17. Re-engage the safety mechanism.
18. Pause for (2) count.
19. Repeat sequences 1-18 (25) times.

Movement 4 (SUL Ready)

1. Continually take small steps forward, backward left and right while repeating all sequences of Movements 1-3 (25) times.
2. Repeat all sequences of Movements 1-3 (25) times using a Par-Time Random Beep to initiate simulated fight.
3. Continually take small steps forward, backward left and right while repeating all sequences of Movements 1-3 (25) times using a Par-Time Random Beep to initiate simulated fight.

Holstered

Movement 1 (Holstered)

1. Assure weapon is in Simulated Fire Mode.
2. Perform the following sequences while maintaining complete focus on the Threat and using peripheral vision if needed for the following functions.
3. Acquire Start Position. (i.17a, i.17b, i.17c, i.17d or i.17e)
4. Pause for (2) count.
5. Cognitively think "FIGHT! FIGHT! FIGHT!" while focusing on the Threat.
6. Acquire your Tactical Stance. (i.16)
7. Acquire full holstered grip w/Shooting Hand, disengaging holster snaps and or safeties mechanisms (i.5) at the same time bringing Support Hand to Support Ready Position (i.21a & i.21b)
8. Slowly pull weapon straight up and out of holster (i.6) fluidly acquire Close Ready Position w/F.O.T.G. (i.22a, i.22b & i.3)
9. Inhale slowly and deeply, while slowly extending arms and obtain a two handed grip at a C.Q.B. Ready Position w/F.O.T.G. (i.19a, i.19b & i.3)
10. Acquiring proper grip-tension, disengaging the safety mechanism, while extending arms to Natural Arm Extension, keeping your weapon level, bringing it up to eye-level, while pointing it at the Threat and keeping the Threat in focus. DO NOT DEPRESS TRIGGER (i.7a, i.7b & i.2b)
11. Pause for (2) count.
12. Cognitively think "Assess...Assess...Assess..."
13. Confirm proper Mechanical Alignment (i.1a) If not in Mechanical Alignment, bring weapon into Mechanical Alignment, while cognitively thinking about how your arms and chest feel once in Mechanical Alignment.
14. Memorize the feeling of Mechanical Alignment.
15. Step offline either left or right.
16. Exhale slowly, while relaxing your grip-tension and slowly return to a C.Q.B. Ready Position w/F.O.T.G. (i.19a, i.19b & i.3)
17. Perform an After Action Scan, checking to your right and behind, your left and behind. Visually and cognitively identify a specific object in the process i.e. ABCs Training Aides (i.26a, i.26b, i.26c & i.26d)
18. Pause for (2) count.

19. Return to Close Ready Position w/F.O.T.G. (i.22a, i.22b & i.3)

20. Pause for (2) count.

21. Return weapon to holster and reengage holster snaps and safety mechanisms.

22. Return to same Start Position (i.17a, i.17b, i.17c, i.17d or i.17e)

23. Pause for (2) count.

24. Repeat sequences 1-23 (25) times.

Movement 2 (Holstered)

1. Assure weapon is in Simulated Fire Mode.

2. Perform the following sequences while maintaining complete focus on the Threat and using peripheral vision if needed for the following functions.

3. Acquire Start Position. (i.17a, i.17b, i.17c, i.17d or i.17e)

4. Cognitively think "FIGHT! FIGHT! FIGHT!" while focusing on the Threat.

5. Acquire your Tactical Stance. (i.16)

6. Acquire full holstered grip w/Shooting Hand, disengaging holster snaps and or safeties mechanisms (i.5) at the same time bringing Support Hand to Support Ready Position (i.21a & i.21b)

7. Slowly pull weapon straight up and out of holster (i.6) fluidly acquire Close Ready Position w/F.O.T.G. (i.22a, i.22b & i.3)

8. Inhale slowly and deeply, while slowly extending arms and obtain a two handed grip at a C.Q.B. Ready Position w/F.O.T.G. (i.19a, i.19b & i.3)

9. Acquiring proper grip-tension, disengaging the safety mechanism, placing your trigger finger on the trigger while extending arms to Natural Arm Extension, keeping your weapon level, bringing it up to eye-level, while pointing it at the Threat and keeping the Threat in focus. DO NOT DEPRESS TRIGGER (i.7a, i.7b & i.2b)

10. Pause for (2) count.

11. Cognitively think "Assess...Assess...Assess..."

12. Confirm proper Mechanical Alignment (1.1a) If not in Mechanical Alignment, bring weapon into Mechanical Alignment, while cognitively thinking about how your arms and chest feel once in Mechanical Alignment.

13. Memorize the feeling of Mechanical Alignment.

14. Step offline either left or right.

15. Exhale slowly, while relaxing your grip-tension and slowly return to a C.Q.B. Ready Position w/F.O.T.G. (i.19a, i.19b & i.3)

16. Perform an After Action Scan, checking to your right and behind, your left and behind. Visually and cognitively identify a specific object in the process i.e. ABCs Training Aides (i.26a, i.26b, i.26c & i.26d)

17. Pause for (2) count.

18. Return to Close Ready Position w/F.O.T.G. (i.22a, i.22b & i.3)

19. Pause for (2) count.

20. Re-engage the safety mechanism.

21. Return weapon to holster and reengage holster snaps and safety mechanisms.

22. Return to same Start Position (i.17a, i.17b, i.17c, i.17d or i.17e)

23. Pause for (2) count.

24. Repeat sequences 1-23 (25) times.

Movement 3 (Holstered)

1. Assure weapon is in Simulated Fire Mode.

2. Perform the following sequences while maintaining complete focus on the Threat and using peripheral vision if needed for the following functions.

3. Acquire Start Position. (i.17a, i.17b, i.17c, i.17d or i.17e)

4. Cognitively think "FIGHT! FIGHT! FIGHT!" while focusing on the Threat.

5. Acquire your Tactical Stance. (i.16)

6. Acquire full holstered grip w/Shooting Hand, disengaging holster snaps and or safeties mechanisms (i.5) at the same time bringing Support Hand to Support Ready Position (i.21a & i.21b)

7. Slowly pull weapon straight up and out of holster (i.6) fluidly acquire Close Ready Position w/F.O.T.G. (i.22a, i.22b & i.3)

8. Inhale slowly and deeply, while slowly extending arms and obtain a two handed grip at a C.Q.B. Ready Position w/F.O.T.G. (i.19a, i.19b & i.3)

9. Acquiring proper grip-tension, disengaging the safety mechanism, placing your trigger finger on the trigger while extending arms to Natural Arm Extension, keeping your weapon level, bringing it up to eye-level, while pointing it at the Threat and keeping the Threat in focus while depressing trigger all the way for a simulated fire upon reaching Natural Arm Extension (i.7a, i.7b & i.2b)

10. Pause for (2) while following through.

11. Cognitively think "Assess...Assess...Assess..."

12. Confirm proper Mechanical Alignment (i.1a) If not in Mechanical Alignment, bring weapon into Mechanical Alignment, while cognitively

thinking about how your arms and chest feel once in Mechanical Alignment.

13. Memorize the feeling of Mechanical Alignment.
14. Step offline either left or right.
15. Exhale slowly, while relaxing your grip-tension and slowly return to a C.Q.B. Ready Position w/F.O.T.G. (i.19a, i.19b & i.3)
16. Perform an After Action Scan, checking to your right and behind, your left and behind. Visually and cognitively identify a specific object in the process i.e. ABCs Training Aides (i.26a, i.26b, i.26c & i.26d)
17. Pause for (2) count.
18. Return to Close Ready Position w/F.O.T.G. (i.22a, i.22b & i.3)
19. Pause for (2) count.
20. Rack weapon slide to return to Simulated Fire Mode.
21. Re-engage the safety mechanism.
22. Return weapon to holster and reengage holster snaps and safety mechanisms.
23. Return to very same Start Position (i.17a, i.17b, i.17c, i.17d or i.17e)
24. Pause for (2) count.
25. Repeat sequences 1-24 (25) times.

Movement 4 (Holstered)

1. Continually take small steps forward, backward left and right while repeating all sequences of Movements 1-3 (25) times.
2. Repeat all sequences of Movements 1-3 (25) times using a Par-Time Random Beep to initiate simulated fight.
3. Continually take small steps forward, backward left and right while repeating all sequences of Movements 1-3 (25) times using a Par-Time Random Beep to initiate simulated fight.

Movement 5 (Holstered)

1. Repeat all sequences of Movements 1-3 from each of the other Start Position. (i.17a, i.17b, i.17c, i.17d or i.17e)
2. Continually take small steps forward, backward left and right while repeating all sequences of Movements 1-3 (25) times.
3. Repeat all sequences of Movements 1-3 (25) times using a Par-Time Random Beep to initiate simulated fight.
4. Continually take small steps forward, backward left and right while repeating all sequences of Movements 1-3 (25) times using a Par-Time Random Beep to initiate simulated fight.

Movement 6 (Holstered)
1. Repeat all sequences of Movements 1-3 from each of the other Seated Position. (i.18a, i.18b & i.18c)
2. Repeat all sequences of Movements 1-3 (25) times using a Par-Time Random Beep to initiate simulated fight.

Movement 7 (Holstered)
1. Repeat all sequences of Movements 1-3 from each of the other Seated Position to Tactical Stance. (i.18a, i.18b, i.18c to i.16)
2. Repeat all sequences of Movements 1-3 (25) times using a Par-Time Random Beep to initiate simulated fight.

Tactical Reload - Handgun

Movement 1 (Tactical Reload—Handgun)

1. Assure weapon is in Simulated Fire Mode.
2. Perform the following sequences while maintaining complete focus on the Threat and using peripheral vision if needed for the following functions.
3. Acquire your Tactical Stance. (i.16)
4. Inhale slowly and deeply, while slowly extending arms to Natural Arm Extension, while also acquiring proper grip-tension, disengaging the safety mechanism, placing your trigger finger on the trigger, keep your weapon level, bringing it up to eye-level, while pointing it at the Threat. (i.7a, i.7b & i.2b)
5. Pause for (2) count.
6. Cognitively think "TACTICAL LULL" while focusing on the Threat.
7. Pause for (2) count.
8. Cognitively think "RE-CHARGE"
9. Step offline left or right.
10. Bring arms back to Reload Ready Position w/F.O.T.G. and weapon canted 45° towards ejection port. (i.23a, 1.23b & i.3)
11. Retrieve simulated fresh magazine with Support Hand, staging magazine between your index and middle fingers. (i.10a)
12. While still holding simulated fresh magazine, move Support Hand back to mag-well of weapon.
13. Manipulate magazine release with Shooting Hand dropping simulated partial magazine into you Support Hand between your thumb and index fingers (i.10b)
14. Insert simulated fresh magazine while still holding onto simulated partial magazine.
15. Tap the bottom of the weapon and mag-well w/palm of Support Hand w/generous force. (i.11)
16. Stow simulated partial magazine in waistband or in pocket.
17. Regain two-handed grip of weapon and return to C.Q.B. Ready w/F.O.T.G. (i.19a, i.19b & i.3)
18. Pause for (2) count.
19. Perform an After Action Scan, checking to your right and behind, your left and behind. Visually and cognitively identify a specific object in the process i.e. ABCs Training Aides (i.26a, i.26b, i.26c & i.26d)

20. Pause for (2) count.

21. From C.Q.B. Position Repeat sequences 1-20 (25) times.

Movement 2 (Tactical Reload—Handgun)

1. Continually take small steps forward, backward left and right while repeating all sequences of Movements 1 (25) times.

2. Repeat all sequences of Movements 1 (25) times using a Par-Time Random Beep to initiate simulated fight.

3. Continually take small steps forward, backward left and right while repeating all sequences of Movements 1 (25) times using a Par-Time Random Beep to initiate simulated fight.

Combat Reload - Handgun

Movement 1 (Combat Reload—Handgun)

1. Stage weapon to create an empty chamber with empty magazine and slide locked rearward, i.e. no Snap-Caps.
2. Perform the following sequences while maintaining complete focus on the Threat and using peripheral vision if needed for the following functions.
3. Acquire your Tactical Stance. (i.16)
4. Pause for (2) count.
5. Cognitively think "FIGHT! FIGHT! FIGHT!" while focusing on the Threat.
6. Inhale slowly and deeply, while slowly extending arms to Natural Arm Extension, while also acquiring proper grip-tension, disengaging the safety mechanism, placing your trigger finger on the trigger, keep your weapon level, bringing it up to eye-level, while pointing it at the Threat while keeping the Threat in focus and depressing trigger all the way for a simulated fire upon reaching Natural Arm Extension (i.7a, i.7b & i.2b)
7. WEAPON WON'T FIRE!!!
8. Cognitively think "MALFUNCTION!"
9. Step offline either left or right while slightly canting weapon to briefly assess the ejection port.
10. Visually and cognitively identify an empty weapon.
11. Cognitively think "FEED!"
12. Bring arms back to Reload Ready Position w/F.O.T.G., manipulate magazine release button while stripping and discarding the empty magazine w/weapon tilted 45° towards ejection port. (i.23a, 1.23b & i.3)
13. Retrieve a simulated fresh magazine, i.e. w/Snap-Caps, from holder/pouch/pocket, being sure to index top of magazine w/Support Hand Index Finger. (i.8)
14. Load simulated fresh magazine.
15. Tap the bottom of the weapon and mag-well w/palm of Support Hand w/generous force. (i.11)
16. While sweeping ejection port on the way back with Support Hand, rack the slide rearward to charge weapon and bring it to a Simulated Fire Mode. (i.12a, i.12b, i.12c & i.12d)

17. Cognitively think "FIGHT! FIGHT! FIGHT!" while focusing on the Threat.
18. Inhale slowly and deeply, while slowly extending arms to Natural Arm Extension, while also acquiring proper grip-tension, disengaging the safety mechanism, placing your trigger finger on the trigger, keep your weapon level, bringing it up to eye-level, while pointing it at the Threat while keeping the Threat in focus and depressing trigger all the way for a simulated fire upon reaching Natural Arm Extension (i.7a, i.7b & i.2b)
19. Pause for (2) while following through.
20. Cognitively think "Assess...Assess...Assess..."
21. Confirm proper Mechanical Alignment (i.1a) If not in Mechanical Alignment, bring weapon into Mechanical Alignment, while cognitively thinking about how your arms and chest feel once in Mechanical Alignment.
22. Memorize the feeling of Mechanical Alignment.
23. Step offline either left or right.
24. Exhale slowly, while relaxing your grip-tension and slowly return to a C.Q.B. Ready Position w/F.O.T.G. (i.19a, i.19b & i.3)
25. Perform an After Action Scan, checking to your right and behind, your left and behind. Visually and cognitively identify a specific object in the process i.e. ABCs Training Aides (i.26a, i.26b, i.26c & i.26d)
26. Pause for (2) count.
27. Re-stage weapon to create an empty chamber with empty magazine and slide locked rearward, i.e. no Snap-Caps.
28. Re-engage the safety mechanism.
29. Pause for (2) count.
30. From C.Q.B. Ready Position, repeat sequences 1-29 (25) times.

Movement 2 (Combat Reload—Handgun)

1. Continually take small steps forward, backward left and right while repeating all sequences of Movements 1 (25) times.
2. Repeat all sequences of Movements 1 (25) times using a Par-Time Random Beep to initiate simulated fight.
3. Continually take small steps forward, backward left and right while repeating all sequences of Movements 1 (25) times using a Par-Time Random Beep to initiate simulated fight.

Type 1 Malfunction - Handgun

Movement 1 (Type 1 Malfunction—Handgun)

1. Stage weapon to create an empty chamber with slide locked forward and a simulated full magazine w/ Snap-Caps
2. Perform the following sequences while maintaining complete focus on the Threat and using peripheral vision if needed for the following functions.
3. Acquire your Tactical Stance. (i.16)
4. Pause for (2) count.
5. Cognitively think "FIGHT! FIGHT! FIGHT!" while focusing on the Threat.
6. Inhale slowly and deeply, while slowly extending arms to Natural Arm Extension, while also acquiring proper grip-tension, disengaging the safety mechanism, placing your trigger finger on the trigger, keep your weapon level, bringing it up to eye-level, while pointing it at the Threat while keeping the Threat in focus and depressing trigger all the way for a simulated fire upon reaching Natural Arm Extension (i.7a, i.7b & i.2b)
7. WEAPON WON'T FIRE!!!
8. Cognitively think "MALFUNCTION!"
9. Step offline either left or right while slightly canting weapon to briefly assess the ejection port.
10. Visually and cognitively identify a Type 1 Malfunction.
11. Cognitively think "TAP - RACK - REENGAGE"
12. Bring arms back to Reload Ready Position w/F.O.T.G. w/weapon tilted 45° towards ejection port. (i.23a, 1.23b & i.3)
13. Tap the bottom of the weapon and mag-well w/palm of Support Hand w/generous force. (i.11)
14. While sweeping ejection port on the way back with Support Hand, rack the slide rearward to charge weapon and bring it to a Simulated Fire Mode. (i.12a, i.12b, i.12c & i.12d)
15. Cognitively think "FIGHT! FIGHT! FIGHT!" while focusing on the Threat.
16. Inhale slowly and deeply, while slowly extending arms to Natural Arm Extension, while also acquiring proper grip-tension, disengaging the safety mechanism, placing your trigger finger on the trigger, keep your weapon level, bringing it up to eye-level, while pointing it at the Threat while keeping the Threat in focus and depressing trigger all the way for

a simulated fire upon reaching Natural Arm Extension (i.7a, i.7b & i.2b)

17. Pause for (2) while following through.
18. Cognitively think "Assess...Assess...Assess..."
19. Confirm proper Mechanical Alignment (i.1a) If not in Mechanical Alignment, bring weapon into Mechanical Alignment, while cognitively thinking about how your arms and chest feel once in Mechanical Alignment.
20. Memorize the feeling of Mechanical Alignment.
21. Step offline either left or right.
22. Exhale slowly, while relaxing your grip-tension and slowly return to a C.Q.B. Ready Position w/F.O.T.G. (i.19a, i.19b & i.3)
23. Perform an After Action Scan, checking to your right and behind, your left and behind. Visually and cognitively identify a specific object in the process i.e. ABCs Training Aides (i.26a, i.26b, i.26c & i.26d)
24. Pause for (2) count.
25. Re-stage weapon to create an empty chamber with slide locked forward and a simulated full magazine w/ Snap-Caps
26. Re-engage the safety mechanism.
27. Pause for (2) count.
28. From C.Q.B. Ready Position, repeat sequences 1-27 (25) times.

Movement 2 (Type 1 Malfunction—Handgun)

1. Continually take small steps forward, backward left and right while repeating all sequences of Movements 1 (25) times.
2. Repeat all sequences of Movements 1 (25) times using a Par-Time Random Beep to initiate simulated fight.
3. Continually take small steps forward, backward left and right while repeating all sequences of Movements 1 (25) times using a Par-Time Random Beep to initiate simulated fight.

Type 2 Malfunction - Handgun

Movement 1 (Type 2 Malfunction—Handgun)

1. Stage weapon to create an empty chamber, simulated full magazine and a Type 2 Stovepipe w/ Snap-Caps. (i.13a & i.13b)

2. Perform the following sequences while maintaining complete focus on the Threat and using peripheral vision if needed for the following functions.

3. Acquire your Tactical Stance. (i.16)

4. Pause for (2) count.

5. Cognitively think "FIGHT! FIGHT! FIGHT!" while focusing on the Threat.

6. Inhale slowly and deeply, while slowly extending arms to Natural Arm Extension, while also acquiring proper grip-tension, disengaging the safety mechanism, placing your trigger finger on the trigger, keep your weapon level, bringing it up to eye-level, while pointing it at the Threat while keeping the Threat in focus and depressing trigger all the way for a simulated fire upon reaching Natural Arm Extension (i.7a, i.7b & i.2b)

7. WEAPON WON'T FIRE!!!

8. Cognitively think "MALFUNCTION!"

9. Step offline either left or right while slightly canting weapon to briefly assess the ejection port.

10. Visually and cognitively identify a Type 2 Malfunction.

11. Cognitively think "TAP - SWEEP - RACK - REENGAGE"

12. Bring arms back to Reload Ready Position w/F.O.T.G. w/weapon tilted 45° towards ejection port. (i.23a, 1.23b & i.3)

13. Tap the bottom of the weapon and mag-well w/palm of Support Hand w/generous force. (i.11)

14. While sweeping ejection port on the way back with Support Hand, rack the slide rearward (3) times back and forth to assure the malfunction clears, then charge weapon and bring it to a Simulated Fire Mode. (i.12a, i.12b, i.12c & i.12d)

15. Cognitively think "FIGHT! FIGHT! FIGHT!" while focusing on the Threat.

16. Inhale slowly and deeply, while slowly extending arms to Natural Arm Extension, while also acquiring proper grip-tension, disengaging the safety mechanism, placing your trigger finger on the trigger, keep your weapon level, bringing it up to eye-level, while pointing it at the Threat while keeping the Threat in focus and depressing trigger all the way for

a simulated fire upon reaching Natural Arm Extension (i.7a, i.7b & i.2b)

17. Pause for (2) while following through.
18. Cognitively think "Assess...Assess...Assess..."
19. Confirm proper Mechanical Alignment (i.1a) If not in Mechanical Alignment, bring weapon into Mechanical Alignment, while cognitively thinking about how your arms and chest feel once in Mechanical Alignment.
20. Memorize the feeling of Mechanical Alignment.
21. Step offline either left or right.
22. Exhale slowly, while relaxing your grip-tension and slowly return to a C.Q.B. Ready Position w/F.O.T.G. (i.19a, i.19b & i.3)
23. Perform an After Action Scan, checking to your right and behind, your left and behind. Visually and cognitively identify a specific object in the process i.e. ABCs Training Aides (i.26a, i.26b, i.26c & i.26d)
24. Pause for (2) count.
25. Re-stage weapon to create an empty chamber, simulated full magazine and a Type 2 Stovepipe w/ Snap-Caps. (i.13a & i.13b)
26. Re-engage the safety mechanism.
27. Pause for (2) count.
28. From C.Q.B. Ready Position, repeat sequences 1-27 (25) times.

Movement 2 (Type 2 Malfunction—Handgun)

1. Continually take small steps forward, backward left and right while repeating all sequences of Movements 1 (25) times.
2. Repeat all sequences of Movements 1 (25) times using a Par-Time Random Beep to initiate simulated fight.
3. Continually take small steps forward, backward left and right while repeating all sequences of Movements 1 (25) times using a Par-Time Random Beep to initiate simulated fight.

Type 3 Malfunction - Handgun

Movement 1 (Type 3 Malfunction—Handgun)

1. Stage weapon to create a Type 3 Double-Feed w/ Snap-Caps and a simulated full magazine. (i.14a & i.14b)
2. Perform the following sequences while maintaining complete focus on the Threat and using peripheral vision if needed for the following functions.
3. Acquire your Tactical Stance. (i.16)
4. Pause for (2) count.
5. Cognitively think "FIGHT! FIGHT! FIGHT!" while focusing on the Threat.
6. Inhale slowly and deeply, while slowly extending arms to Natural Arm Extension, while also acquiring proper grip-tension, disengaging the safety mechanism, placing your trigger finger on the trigger, keep your weapon level, bringing it up to eye-level, while pointing it at the Threat while keeping the Threat in focus and depressing trigger all the way for a simulated fire upon reaching Natural Arm Extension (i.7a, i.7b & i.2b)
7. WEAPON WON'T FIRE!!!
8. Cognitively think "MALFUNCTION!"
9. Step offline either left or right while slightly canting weapon to briefly assess the ejection port.
10. Visually and cognitively identify a Type 3 Malfunction.
11. Cognitively think "STRIP - RACK - FEED - TAP - RACK - REENGAGE"
12. Bring arms back to Reload Ready Position w/F.O.T.G. w/weapon tilted 45° towards ejection port. (i.23a, 1.23b & i.3)
13. Manipulate magazine release button and forcefully strip magazine clear from weapon. (If you have an extra magazine, discard stripped magazine otherwise retain it)
14. While sweeping ejection port on the way back with Support Hand, rack the slide rearward (3) times back and forth to assure the malfunction clears. (i.12a, i.12b, i.12c & i.12d)
15. Retrieve a simulated fresh magazine, i.e. w/Snap-Caps, from holder/pouch/pocket, being sure to index top of magazine w/Support Hand Index Finger. (i.8)
16. Load simulated fresh magazine.
17. Tap the bottom of the weapon and mag-well w/palm of Support Hand w/generous force. (i.11)

18. While sweeping ejection port on the way back with Support Hand, rack the slide rearward to charge weapon and bring it to a Simulated Fire Mode. (i.12a, i.12b, i.12c & i.12d)

19. Cognitively think "FIGHT! FIGHT! FIGHT!" while focusing on the Threat.

20. Inhale slowly and deeply, while slowly extending arms to Natural Arm Extension, while also acquiring proper grip-tension, disengaging the safety mechanism, placing your trigger finger on the trigger, keep your weapon level, bringing it up to eye-level, while pointing it at the Threat while keeping the Threat in focus and depressing trigger all the way for a simulated fire upon reaching Natural Arm Extension (i.7a, i.7b & i.2b)

21. Pause for (2) while following through.

22. Cognitively think "Assess...Assess...Assess..."

23. Confirm proper Mechanical Alignment (i.1a) If not in Mechanical Alignment, bring weapon into Mechanical Alignment, while cognitively thinking about how your arms and chest feel once in Mechanical Alignment.

24. Memorize the feeling of Mechanical Alignment.

25. Step offline either left or right.

26. Exhale slowly, while relaxing your grip-tension and slowly return to a C.Q.B. Ready Position w/F.O.T.G. (i.19a, i.19b & i.3)

27. Perform an After Action Scan, checking to your right and behind, your left and behind. Visually and cognitively identify a specific object in the process i.e. ABCs Training Aides (i.26a, i.26b, i.26c & i.26d)

28. Pause for (2) count.

29. Re-stage weapon to create a Type 3 Double-Feed w/ Snap-Caps and a simulated full magazine. (i.14a & i.14b)

30. Re-engage the safety mechanism.

31. Pause for (2) count.

32. From C.Q.B. Ready Position, repeat sequences 1-31 (25) times.

Movement 2 (Type 3 Malfunction—Handgun)

1. Continually take small steps forward, backward left and right while repeating all sequences of Movements 1 (25) times.

2. Repeat all sequences of Movements 1 (25) times using a Par-Time Random Beep to initiate simulated fight.

3. Continually take small steps forward, backward left and right while repeating all sequences of Movements 1 (25) times using a Par-Time Random Beep to initiate simulated fight.

Decreasing Par-Time Drills Handgun

These drills are best accomplished using a shooting par-timer

C.Q.B. Ready (Par-Time Speed)

Movement 1

Assure weapon is in Simulated Fire Mode and perform the following steps while maintaining complete focus on the Threat and using peripheral vision if needed for the following functions.

1. Acquire a C.Q.B. Ready Position w/F.O.T.G.

START BEEP...

2. Cognitively think "FIGHT! FIGHT! FIGHT!" while maintaining focus on the Threat, inhale slowly and deeply, while slowly extending arms to Natural Arm Extension, while also acquiring proper grip-tension, disengaging the safety mechanism, placing your trigger finger on the trigger, keep your weapon level, bringing it up to eye-level, while pointing it at the Threat while keeping the Threat in focus and depressing trigger all the way for a simulated fire upon reaching Natural Arm Extension.

END BEEP...

3. Pause for (2) while following through, cognitively think "Assess...Assess...Assess..."
4. Confirm proper Mechanical Alignment. If not in Mechanical Alignment, bring weapon into Mechanical Alignment, while cognitively thinking about how your arms and chest feel once in Mechanical Alignment.
5. Memorize the feeling of Mechanical Alignment.
6. Step offline either left or right, exhale slowly, while relaxing your grip-tension and slowly return to a C.Q.B. Ready Position w/F.O.T.G., perform an After Action Scan, checking to your right and behind, your left and behind. Visually and cognitively identify a specific object in the process i.e. ABCs Training Aides.
7. Pause for (2) count.
8. Rack weapon slide to return to Simulated Fire Mode.
9. Re-engage the safety mechanism.
10. Pause for (2) count.
11. Repeat sequences 1-10 (25) times.

Movement 2

1. Reset Par-Timer and Repeat (25) Times with-in 2 seconds.

Movement 3

1. Reset Par-Timer and Repeat (25) Times with-in 1.5 seconds.

Movement 4

1. Reset Par-Timer and Repeat (25) Times with-in 1.3 seconds.

Movement 5

1. Reset Par-Timer and Repeat (25) Times with-in 0.9 seconds.

Movement 6

1. Reset Par-Timer and repeat (25) Times with-in 0.8 seconds.

Movement 7

1. Reset Par-Timer, continually take small steps forward, backward left, right and repeat Movements 1-6 (25) times.

SUL Ready (Par-Time Speed)

Movement 1

Assure weapon is in Simulated Fire Mode and perform the following steps while maintaining complete focus on the Threat and using peripheral vision if needed for the following functions.

1. Acquire a SUL Ready Position w/F.O.T.G.

START BEEP...

2. Cognitively think "FIGHT! FIGHT! FIGHT!" while maintaining focus on the Threat, inhale slowly and deeply, while slowly extending arms to Natural Arm Extension, while also acquiring proper grip-tension, disengaging the safety mechanism, placing your trigger finger on the trigger, keep your weapon level, bringing it up to eye-level, while pointing it at the Threat while keeping the Threat in focus and depressing trigger all the way for a simulated fire upon reaching Natural Arm Extension

END BEEP...

3. Pause for (2) while following through, cognitively think "Assess...Assess...Assess..."
4. Confirm proper Mechanical Alignment. If not in Mechanical Alignment, bring weapon into Mechanical Alignment, while cognitively thinking about how your arms and chest feel once in Mechanical Alignment.
5. Memorize the feeling of Mechanical Alignment.
6. Step offline either left or right, exhale slowly, while relaxing your grip-tension and slowly return to a SUL Ready Position w/F.O.T.G. perform an After Action Scan, checking to your right and behind, your left and behind. Visually and cognitively identify a specific object in the process i.e. ABCs Training Aides.
7. Pause for (2) count.
8. Rack weapon slide to return to Simulated Fire Mode.
9. Re-engage the safety mechanism.
10. Pause for (2) count.
11. Repeat sequences 1-10 (25) times.

Movement 2

1. Reset Par-Timer and Repeat (25) Times with-in 2 seconds.

Movement 3

1. Reset Par-Timer and Repeat (25) Times with-in 1.5 seconds.

Movement 4

1. Reset Par-Timer and Repeat (25) Times with-in 1.3 seconds.

Movement 5

1. Reset Par-Timer and Repeat (25) Times with-in 0.9 seconds.

Movement 6

1. Reset Par-Timer and repeat (25) Times with-in 0.8 seconds.

Movement 7

1. Reset Par-Timer, continually take small steps forward, backward left, right and repeat Movements 1-6 (25) times.

Holstered (Par-Time Speed)

Movement 1

Assure weapon is in Simulated Fire Mode and perform the following steps while maintaining complete focus on the Threat and using peripheral vision if needed for the following functions.

1. Acquire your Tactical Stance and wait for beep.

START BEEP...

2. Cognitively think "FIGHT! FIGHT! FIGHT!" while maintaining focus on the Threat, acquire full holstered grip w/Shooting Hand, disengaging holster snaps and or safeties mechanisms at the same time bringing Support Hand to Support Ready Position slowly pull weapon straight up and out of holster fluidly acquire Close Ready Position w/F.O.T.G. inhale slowly and deeply, while slowly extending arms and obtain a two handed grip at a C.Q.B. Ready Position w/F.O.T.G. acquiring proper grip-tension, disengaging the safety mechanism, placing your trigger finger on the trigger while extending arms to Natural Arm Extension, keeping your weapon level, bringing it up to eye-level, while pointing it at the Threat and keeping the Threat in focus while depressing trigger all the way for a simulated fire upon reaching Natural Arm Extension

END BEEP...

3. Pause for (2) while following through, cognitively think "Assess...Assess...Assess..."
4. Confirm proper Mechanical Alignment. If not in Mechanical Alignment, bring weapon into Mechanical Alignment, while cognitively thinking about how your arms and chest feel once in Mechanical Alignment.
5. Memorize the feeling of Mechanical Alignment.
6. Step offline either left or right, exhale slowly, while relaxing your grip-tension and slowly return to a C.Q.B. Ready Position w/F.O.T.G. perform an After Action Scan, checking to your right and behind, your left and behind. Visually and cognitively identify a specific object in the process i.e. ABCs Training Aides.
7. Pause for (2) count.
8. Return to Close Ready Position w/F.O.T.G. (i.22a, i.22b & i.3)
9. Pause for (2) count.
10. Rack weapon slide to return to Simulated Fire Mode.
11. Re-engage the safety mechanism.
12. Return weapon to holster and reengage holster snaps and safety mechanisms.

13. Repeat sequences 1-12 (25) times.

Movement 2

1. Reset Par-Timer and Repeat (25) Times with-in 2 seconds.

Movement 3

1. Reset Par-Timer and Repeat (25) Times with-in 1.5 seconds.

Movement 4

1. Reset Par-Timer and Repeat (25) Times with-in 1.3 seconds.

Movement 5

1. Reset Par-Timer and Repeat (25) Times with-in 0.9 seconds.

Movement 6

1. Reset Par-Timer and repeat (25) Times with-in 0.8 seconds.

Movement 7

1. Reset Par-Timer, continually take small steps forward, backward left, right and repeat Movements 1-6 (25) times.

Seated (Par-Time Speed)

Movement 1

Assure weapon is in Simulated Fire Mode and perform the following steps while maintaining complete focus on the Threat and using peripheral vision if needed for the following functions.

1. Acquire a Seated Position and wait for beep.

START BEEP...

2. Cognitively think "FIGHT! FIGHT! FIGHT!" while maintaining focus on the Threat, acquire full holstered grip w/Shooting Hand, disengaging holster snaps and or safeties mechanisms at the same time bringing Support Hand to Support Ready Position slowly pull weapon straight up and out of holster fluidly acquire Close Ready Position w/F.O.T.G. inhale slowly and deeply, while slowly extending arms and obtain a two handed grip at a C.Q.B. Ready Position w/F.O.T.G. acquiring proper grip-tension, disengaging the safety mechanism, placing your trigger finger on the trigger while extending arms to Natural Arm Extension, keeping your weapon level, bringing it up to eye-level, while pointing it at the Threat and keeping the Threat in focus while depressing trigger all the way for a simulated fire upon reaching Natural Arm Extension

END BEEP...

3. Pause for (2) while following through, cognitively think "Assess...Assess...Assess..."
4. Confirm proper Mechanical Alignment. If not in Mechanical Alignment, bring weapon into Mechanical Alignment, while cognitively thinking about how your arms and chest feel once in Mechanical Alignment.
5. Memorize the feeling of Mechanical Alignment.
6. Step offline either left or right, exhale slowly, while relaxing your grip-tension and slowly return to a C.Q.B. Ready Position w/F.O.T.G. perform an After Action Scan, checking to your right and behind, your left and behind. Visually and cognitively identify a specific object in the process i.e. ABCs Training Aides.
7. Pause for (2) count.
8. Return to Close Ready Position w/F.O.T.G.
9. Pause for (2) count.
10. Rack weapon slide to return to Simulated Fire Mode.
11. Re-engage the safety mechanism.
12. Return weapon to holster and reengage holster snaps and safety mechanisms.

13. Repeat sequences 1-12 (25) times.

Movement 2

1. Reset Par-Timer and Repeat (25) Times with-in 2 seconds.

Movement 3

1. Reset Par-Timer and Repeat (25) Times with-in 1.5 seconds.

Movement 4

1. Reset Par-Timer and Repeat (25) Times with-in 1.3 seconds.

Movement 5

1. Reset Par-Timer and Repeat (25) Times with-in 0.9 seconds.

Movement 6

1. Reset Par-Timer and repeat (25) Times with-in 0.8 seconds.

Movement 7

1. Reset Par-Timer, continually take small steps forward, backward left, right and repeat Movements 1-6 (25) times.

Seated to Tactical Stance
(Par-Time Speed)

Movement 1

Assure weapon is in Simulated Fire Mode and perform the following steps while maintaining complete focus on the Threat and using peripheral vision if needed for the following functions.

1. Acquire a Seated Position and wait for beep.

START BEEP...

2. Cognitively think "FIGHT! FIGHT! FIGHT!" while maintaining focus on the Threat, acquire Tactical Stance acquire full holstered grip w/Shooting Hand, disengaging holster snaps and or safeties mechanisms at the same time bringing Support Hand to Support Ready Position slowly pull weapon straight up and out of holster fluidly acquire Close Ready Position w/F.O.T.G. inhale slowly and deeply, while slowly extending arms and obtain a two handed grip at a C.Q.B. Ready Position w/F.O.T.G. acquiring proper grip-tension, disengaging the safety mechanism, placing your trigger finger on the trigger while extending arms to Natural Arm Extension, keeping your weapon level, bringing it up to eye-level, while pointing it at the Threat and keeping the Threat in focus while depressing trigger all the way for a simulated fire upon reaching Natural Arm Extension

END BEEP...

3. Pause for (2) while following through, cognitively think "Assess...Assess...Assess..."
4. Confirm proper Mechanical Alignment If not in Mechanical Alignment, bring weapon into Mechanical Alignment, while cognitively thinking about how your arms and chest feel once in Mechanical Alignment.
5. Memorize the feeling of Mechanical Alignment.
6. Step offline either left or right, exhale slowly, while relaxing your grip-tension and slowly return to a C.Q.B. Ready Position w/F.O.T.G. perform an After Action Scan, checking to your right and behind, your left and behind. Visually and cognitively identify a specific object in the process i.e. ABCs Training Aides.
7. Pause for (2) count.
8. Return to Close Ready Position w/F.O.T.G.
9. Pause for (2) count.
10. Rack weapon slide to return to Simulated Fire Mode.

11. Re-engage the safety mechanism.
12. Return weapon to holster and reengage holster snaps and safety mechanisms.
13. Repeat sequences 1-12 (25) times.

Movement 2

1. Reset Par-Timer and Repeat (25) Times with-in 2 seconds.

Movement 3

1. Reset Par-Timer and Repeat (25) Times with-in 1.5 seconds.

Movement 4

1. Reset Par-Timer and Repeat (25) Times with-in 1.3 seconds.

Movement 5

1. Reset Par-Timer and Repeat (25) Times with-in 0.9 seconds.

Movement 6

1. Reset Par-Timer and repeat (25) Times with-in 0.8 seconds.

Movement 7

1. Reset Par-Timer, continually take small steps forward, backward left, right and repeat Movements 1-6 (25) times.

Tactical Reload - Handgun
(Par-Time Speed)

Movement 1

Assure weapon is in Simulated Fire Mode and perform the following steps while maintaining complete focus on the Threat and using peripheral vision if needed for the following functions.

1. Acquire your Tactical Stance. with two handed grip and arms at Natural Arm Extension with trigger finger on the trigger while pointing weapon at the Threat and wait for beep.

START BEEP...

2. Cognitively think "TACTICAL LULL" while focusing on the Threat, then cognitively think "RE-CHARGE", stepping offline to your right or left, bringing arms back to Reload Ready Position w/F.O.T.G. and weapon canted 45° towards ejection port. Retrieve simulated fresh magazine with support-hand and, staging magazine between your index and middle fingers, while still holding simulated fresh magazine, move support-hand back to mag-well of weapon, while manipulating magazine release with Shooting Hand to drop simulated partial magazine into you support-hand and between your thumb and index fingers, insert simulated fresh magazine while still holding onto simulated partial magazine, tap the bottom of the weapon and mag-well w/palm of support-hand w/generous force., stow simulated partial magazine in waistband or in pocket, regain two-handed grip of weapon and return to C.Q.B. Ready w/F.O.T.G.

END BEEP...

3. Pause for (2) while following through, cognitively think "Assess...Assess...Assess..."

4. Confirm proper Mechanical Sight Alignment. If not in Mechanical Alignment, bring weapon into Mechanical Alignment, while cognitively thinking about how your arms and chest feel once in Mechanical Alignment.

5. Memorize the feeling of Mechanical Alignment.

6. Step offline to your right or left, exhale slowly, while relaxing your grip-tension and slowly return to a C.Q.B. Ready Position w/F.O.T.G., perform an After Action Scan, checking to your right and behind, your left and behind. Visually and cognitively identify an ABCs training placard and describe it aloud i.e. Blue, Square, Alpha.

7. Pause for (2) count.

8. Re-engage the safety mechanism.
9. Repeat sequences 1-8 (25) times.

Movement 2

1. Reset Par-Timer and Repeat (25) Times with-in 2 seconds.

Movement 3

1. Reset Par-Timer and Repeat (25) Times with-in 1.5 seconds.

Movement 4

1. Reset Par-Timer and Repeat (25) Times with-in 1.3 seconds.

Movement 5

1. Reset Par-Timer and Repeat (25) Times with-in 0.9 seconds.

Movement 6

1. Reset Par-Timer and repeat (25) Times with-in 0.8 seconds.

Movement 7

1. Reset Par-Timer, continually take small steps forward, backward left, right and repeat Movements 1-6 (25) times.

Combat Reload - Handgun
(Par-Time Speed)

Movement 1

Assure weapon is staged to create an empty chamber with empty magazine and slide locked rearward, i.e. no Snap-Cap, then perform the following steps while maintaining complete focus on the Threat and using peripheral vision if needed for the following functions.

1. Acquire your Tactical Stance. with two handed grip and arms at Natural Arm Extension with trigger finger on the trigger while pointing weapon at the Threat and wait for beep.

START BEEP...

2. Cognitively think "FIGHT! FIGHT! FIGHT!" while focusing on the Threat, depressing trigger all the way for a simulated fire. WEAPON WON'T FIRE!!! cognitively think "MALFUNCTION!" step offline to your left, while slightly canting weapon to briefly assess the ejection port, visually and cognitively identify an empty weapon, cognitively think "FEED!" bring arms back to Reload Ready Position w/F.O.T.G., manipulate magazine release button while stripping and discarding the empty magazine w/weapon tilted 45° towards ejection port, retrieve a simulated fresh magazine, being sure to index top of magazine w/support-hand and Index Finger, load simulated fresh magazine, tap the bottom of the weapon and mag-well w/palm of support-hand w/generous force, while sweeping ejection port on the way back with support-hand, rack the slide rearward to charge weapon and bring it to a Simulated Fire Mode, cognitively think "FIGHT! FIGHT! FIGHT!" while focusing on the Threat. inhale slowly and deeply, while slowly extending arms to Natural Arm Extension, while also acquiring proper grip-tension, keep your weapon level, bringing it up to eye-level, while pointing it at the Threat and keeping the Threat in focus and depressing trigger all the way for a simulated fire upon reaching Natural Arm Extension

END BEEP...

3. Pause for (2) while following through, cognitively think "Assess...Assess...Assess..."
4. Confirm proper Mechanical Sight Alignment. If not in Mechanical Alignment, bring weapon into Mechanical Alignment, while cognitively thinking about how your arms and chest feel once in Mechanical Alignment.
5. Memorize the feeling of Mechanical Alignment.

6. Step offline to your right or left, exhale slowly, while relaxing your grip-tension and slowly return to a C.Q.B. Ready Position w/F.O.T.G., perform an After Action Scan, checking to your right and behind, your left and behind. Visually and cognitively identify an ABCs training placard and describe it aloud i.e. Blue, Square, Alpha.
7. Pause for (2) count.
8. Re-engage the safety mechanism.
9. Repeat sequences 1-8 (25) times.

Movement 2

1. Reset Par-Timer and Repeat (25) Times with-in 2 seconds.

Movement 3

1. Reset Par-Timer and Repeat (25) Times with-in 1.5 seconds.

Movement 4

1. Reset Par-Timer and Repeat (25) Times with-in 1.3 seconds.

Movement 5

1. Reset Par-Timer and Repeat (25) Times with-in 0.9 seconds.

Movement 6

1. Reset Par-Timer and repeat (25) Times with-in 0.8 seconds.

Movement 7

1. Reset Par-Timer, continually take small steps forward, backward left, right and repeat Movements 1-6 (25) times.

Type 1 Malfunction - Handgun
(Par-Time Speed)

Movement 1

Assure weapon is staged to create an empty chamber with slide locked forward and a simulated full magazine w/ Snap-Caps, then perform the following steps while maintaining complete focus on the Threat and using peripheral vision if needed for the following functions.

1. Acquire your Tactical Stance with two handed grip and arms at Natural Arm Extension with trigger finger on the trigger while pointing weapon at the Threat and wait for beep.

START BEEP...

2. Cognitively think "FIGHT! FIGHT! FIGHT!" while focusing on the Threat, depressing trigger all the way for a simulated fire. WEAPON WON'T FIRE!!! cognitively think "MALFUNCTION!" step offline to your left, while slightly canting weapon to briefly assess the ejection port, visually and cognitively identify a Type 1 Malfunction, cognitively think "TAP - RACK - REENGAGE" bring arms back to Reload Ready Position w/F.O.T.G. w/weapon tilted 45° towards ejection port, tap the bottom of the weapon and mag-well w/palm of support-hand w/generous force, while sweeping ejection port on the way back with Support Hand, rack the slide rearward to charge weapon and bring it to a simulated Fire Mode, cognitively think "FIGHT! FIGHT! FIGHT!" while focusing on the Threat. inhale slowly and deeply, while slowly extending arms to Natural Arm Extension, while also acquiring proper grip-tension, keep your weapon level, bringing it up to eye-level, while pointing it at the Threat and keeping the Threat in focus and depressing trigger all the way for a simulated fire upon reaching Natural Arm Extension

END BEEP...

3. Pause for (2) while following through, cognitively think "Assess...Assess...Assess..."

4. Confirm proper Mechanical Sight Alignment. If not in Mechanical Alignment, bring weapon into Mechanical Alignment, while cognitively thinking about how your arms and chest feel once in Mechanical Alignment.

5. Memorize the feeling of Mechanical Alignment.

6. Step offline to your right or left, exhale slowly, while relaxing your grip-tension and slowly return to a C.Q.B. Ready Position w/F.O.T.G.,

perform an After Action Scan, checking to your right and behind, your left and behind. Visually and cognitively identify an ABCs training placard and describe it aloud i.e. Blue, Square, Alpha.

7. Pause for (2) count.
8. Re-engage the safety mechanism.
9. Repeat sequences 1-8 (25) times.

Movement 2

1. Reset Par-Timer and Repeat (25) Times with-in 2 seconds.

Movement 3

1. Reset Par-Timer and Repeat (25) Times with-in 1.5 seconds.

Movement 4

1. Reset Par-Timer and Repeat (25) Times with-in 1.3 seconds.

Movement 5

1. Reset Par-Timer and Repeat (25) Times with-in 0.9 seconds.

Movement 6

1. Reset Par-Timer and repeat (25) Times with-in 0.8 seconds.

Movement 7

1. Reset Par-Timer, continually take small steps forward, backward left, right and repeat Movements 1-6 (25) times.

Type 2 Malfunction – Handgun
(Par-Time Speed)

Movement 1

Assure weapon is staged to create an empty chamber, simulated full magazine and a Type 2 Stovepipe w/ Snap-Caps, then perform the following steps while maintaining complete focus on the Threat and using peripheral vision if needed for the following functions.

1. Acquire your Tactical Stance with two handed grip and arms at Natural Arm Extension with trigger finger on the trigger while pointing weapon at the Threat and wait for beep.

START BEEP...

2. Cognitively think "FIGHT! FIGHT! FIGHT!" while focusing on the Threat, depressing trigger all the way for a simulated fire. WEAPON WON'T FIRE!!! cognitively think "MALFUNCTION!" step offline to your left, while slightly canting weapon to briefly assess the ejection port, visually and cognitively identify a Type 2 Malfunction, cognitively think "TAP - RACK - REENGAGE" bring arms back to Reload Ready Position w/F.O.T.G. w/weapon tilted 45° towards ejection port, tap the bottom of the weapon and mag-well w/palm of support-hand w/generous force, while sweeping ejection port on the way back with Support Hand, rack the slide rearward to charge weapon and bring it to a simulated Fire Mode, cognitively think "FIGHT! FIGHT! FIGHT!" while focusing on the Threat. inhale slowly and deeply, while slowly extending arms to Natural Arm Extension, while also acquiring proper grip-tension, keep your weapon level, bringing it up to eye-level, while pointing it at the Threat and keeping the Threat in focus and depressing trigger all the way for a simulated fire upon reaching Natural Arm Extension

END BEEP...

3. Pause for (2) while following through, cognitively think "Assess...Assess...Assess..."
4. Confirm proper Mechanical Sight Alignment. If not in Mechanical Alignment, bring weapon into Mechanical Alignment, while cognitively thinking about how your arms and chest feel once in Mechanical Alignment.
5. Memorize the feeling of Mechanical Alignment.
6. Step offline to your right or left, exhale slowly, while relaxing your grip-tension and slowly return to a C.Q.B. Ready Position w/F.O.T.G.,

perform an After Action Scan, checking to your right and behind, your left and behind. Visually and cognitively identify an ABCs training placard and describe it aloud i.e. Blue, Square, Alpha.

7. Pause for (2) count.
8. Re-engage the safety mechanism.
9. Repeat sequences 1-8 (25) times.

Movement 2

1. Reset Par-Timer and Repeat (25) Times with-in 2 seconds.

Movement 3

1. Reset Par-Timer and Repeat (25) Times with-in 1.5 seconds.

Movement 4

1. Reset Par-Timer and Repeat (25) Times with-in 1.3 seconds.

Movement 5

1. Reset Par-Timer and Repeat (25) Times with-in 0.9 seconds.

Movement 6

1. Reset Par-Timer and repeat (25) Times with-in 0.8 seconds.

Movement 7

1. Reset Par-Timer, continually take small steps forward, backward left, right and repeat Movements 1-6 (25) times.

Type 3 Malfunction – Handgun
(Par-Time Speed)

Movement 1

Assure weapon is staged to create a Type 3 Double-Feed w/ Snap-Caps and a simulated full magazine, then perform the following steps while maintaining complete focus on the Threat and using peripheral vision if needed for the following functions.

1. Acquire your Tactical Stance, with two handed grip and arms at Natural Arm Extension with trigger finger on the trigger while pointing weapon at the Threat and wait for beep.

START BEEP...

2. Cognitively think "FIGHT! FIGHT! FIGHT!" while focusing on the Threat, depressing trigger all the way for a simulated fire. WEAPON WON'T FIRE!!! Cognitively think "STRIP - RACK - FEED - TAP - RACK - REENGAGE", bring arms back to Reload Ready Position w/F.O.T.G. w/weapon tilted 45° towards ejection port, manipulate mag release button and forcefully strip mag clear from weapon, while sweeping ejection port on the way back with support-hand, rack the slide rearward (3) times back and forth to assure the malfunction clears, reinsert mag, being sure to index top of magazine w/support-hand Index finger, tap the bottom of the weapon and mag-well w/palm of support-hand w/generous force, while sweeping ejection port on the way back with support-hand, rack the slide rearward to charge weapon and bring it to a simulated Fire Mode, cognitively think "FIGHT! FIGHT! FIGHT!" while focusing on the Threat. inhale slowly and deeply, while slowly extending arms to Natural Arm Extension, while also acquiring proper grip-tension, keep your weapon level, bringing it up to eye-level, while pointing it at the Threat and keeping the Threat in focus and depressing trigger all the way for a simulated fire upon reaching Natural Arm Extension

END BEEP...

3. Pause for (2) while following through, cognitively think "Assess...Assess...Assess..."

4. Confirm proper Mechanical Sight Alignment. If not in Mechanical Alignment, bring weapon into Mechanical Alignment, while cognitively thinking about how your arms and chest feel once in Mechanical Alignment.

5. Memorize the feeling of Mechanical Alignment.

6. Step offline to your right or left, exhale slowly, while relaxing your grip-tension and slowly return to a C.Q.B. Ready Position w/F.O.T.G., perform an After Action Scan, checking to your right and behind, your left and behind. Visually and cognitively identify an ABCs training placard and describe it aloud i.e. Blue, Square, Alpha.
7. Pause for (2) count.
8. Re-engage the safety mechanism.
9. Repeat sequences 1-8 (25) times.

Movement 2

1. Reset Par-Timer and Repeat (25) Times with-in 2 seconds.

Movement 3

1. Reset Par-Timer and Repeat (25) Times with-in 1.5 seconds.

Movement 4

1. Reset Par-Timer and Repeat (25) Times with-in 1.3 seconds.

Movement 5

1. Reset Par-Timer and Repeat (25) Times with-in 0.9 seconds.

Movement 6

1. Reset Par-Timer and repeat (25) Times with-in 0.8 seconds.

Movement 7

1. Reset Par-Timer, continually take small steps forward, backward left, right and repeat Movements 1-6 (25) times.

LONG GUN

ABSOLUTELY NO AMMUNITION!!!

Index Ready

Movement 1 (Index Ready)

1. Assure weapon is in Simulated Fire Mode.
2. Perform the following sequences while maintaining complete focus on the Threat and using peripheral vision if needed for the following functions.
3. Acquire your Tactical Stance allowing Long Gun to hang slung (i.16)
4. Pause for (2) count.
5. Acquire Index Ready Position w/F.O.T.G. (i.24a & i.24b)
6. Pause for (2) count.
7. Cognitively think "FIGHT! FIGHT! FIGHT!" while focusing on the Threat.
8. Inhale slowly and deeply, while slowly extending arms to Natural Cradle Rest using toe of Long Gun as a pivot point, while also acquiring proper grip-tension, disengaging the safety mechanism, placing trigger finger on the trigger, keep your weapon level, pivoting weapon up to eye-level and into proper cheek-weld, while pointing it at the Threat while keeping the Threat in focus. DO NOT DEPRESS TRIGGER (i.15 & i.27e)
9. Pause for (2) count.
10. Cognitively think "Assess...Assess...Assess..."
11. Confirm proper Mechanical Alignment (i.1b) If not in Mechanical Alignment, bring weapon into Mechanical Alignment, while cognitively thinking about how your arms and chest feel once in Mechanical Alignment.
12. Memorize the feeling of Mechanical Alignment.
13. Step offline either left or right.
14. Exhale slowly, while relaxing your grip-tension and slowly return to an Index Ready Position w/F.O.T.G. (i.24a & i.24b)
15. Perform an After Action Scan, checking to your right and behind, your left and behind. Visually and cognitively identify a specific object in the process i.e. ABCs Training Aides (i.26a, i.26b, i.26c & i.26d)
16. Re-engaging safety mechanism
17. Pause for (2) count.
18. Repeat sequences 1-17 (25) times.

Movement 2 (Index Ready)

1. Assure weapon is in Simulated Fire Mode.

2. Perform the following sequences while maintaining complete focus on the Threat and using peripheral vision if needed for the following functions.

3. Acquire your Tactical Stance allowing Long Gun to hang slung (i.16)

4. Pause for (2) count.

5. Acquire Index Ready Position w/F.O.T.G. (i.24a & i.24b)

6. Pause for (2) count.

7. Cognitively think "FIGHT! FIGHT! FIGHT!" while focusing on the Threat.

8. Inhale slowly and deeply, while slowly extending arms to Natural Cradle Rest using toe of Long Gun as a pivot point, while also acquiring proper grip-tension, disengaging the safety mechanism, placing trigger finger on the trigger, keep your weapon level, pivoting weapon up to eye-level and into proper cheek-weld, while pointing it at the Threat while keeping the Threat in focus. DO NOT DEPRESS TRIGGER. (i.15 & i.27e)

9. Pause for (2) count.

10. Cognitively think "Assess...Assess...Assess..."

11. Confirm proper Mechanical Alignment (i.1b) If not in Mechanical Alignment, bring weapon into Mechanical Alignment, while cognitively thinking about how your arms and chest feel once in Mechanical Alignment.

12. Memorize the feeling of Mechanical Alignment.

13. Step offline either left or right.

14. Exhale slowly, while relaxing your grip-tension and slowly return to an Index Ready Position w/F.O.T.G. (i.24a & i.24b)

15. Perform an After Action Scan, checking to your right and behind, your left and behind. Visually and cognitively identify a specific object in the process i.e. ABCs Training Aides (i.26a, i.26b, i.26c & i.26d)

16. Re-engaging safety mechanism

17. Pause for (2) count.

18. Repeat sequences 1-17 (25) times.

Movement 3 (Index Ready)

1. Assure weapon is in Simulated Fire Mode.

2. Perform the following sequences while maintaining complete focus on the Threat and using peripheral vision if needed for the following functions.

3. Acquire your Tactical Stance allowing Long Gun to hang slung (i.16)

4. Pause for (2) count.

5. Acquire Index Ready Position w/F.O.T.G. (i.24a & i.24b)

6. Pause for (2) count.
7. Cognitively think "FIGHT! FIGHT! FIGHT!" while focusing on the Threat.
8. Inhale slowly and deeply, while slowly extending arms to Natural Cradle Rest using toe of Long Gun as a pivot point, while also acquiring proper grip-tension, disengaging the safety mechanism, placing your trigger finger on the trigger, keep your weapon level, bringing it up to eye-level, while pointing it at the Threat while keeping the Threat in focus and depressing trigger all the way for a simulated fire upon reaching proper cheek-weld (i.15 & i.27e)
9. Pause for (2) count and follow through.
10. Cognitively think "Assess...Assess...Assess..."
11. Confirm proper Mechanical Alignment (i.1b) If not in Mechanical Alignment, bring weapon into Mechanical Alignment, while cognitively thinking about how your arms and chest feel once in Mechanical Alignment.
12. Memorize the feeling of Mechanical Alignment.
13. Step offline either left or right.
14. Exhale slowly, while relaxing your grip-tension and slowly return to an Index Ready Position w/F.O.T.G. (i.24a & i.24b)
15. Perform an After Action Scan, checking to your right and behind, your left and behind. Visually and cognitively identify a specific object in the process i.e. ABCs Training Aides (i.26a, i.26b, i.26c & i.26d)
16. Re-engaging safety mechanism
17. Pause for (2) count.
18. Repeat sequences 1-17 (25) times.

Movement 4 (Index Ready)

1. Continually take small steps forward, backward left and right while repeating all sequences of Movements 1-3 (25) times.
2. Repeat all sequences of Movements 1-3 (25) times using a Par-Time Random Beep to initiate simulated fight.
3. Continually take small steps forward, backward left and right while repeating all sequences of Movements 1-3 (25) times using a Par-Time Random Beep to initiate simulated fight.

Low Index Ready

Movement 1 (Low Index Ready)

1. Assure weapon is in Simulated Fire Mode.
2. Perform the following sequences while maintaining complete focus on the Threat and using peripheral vision if needed for the following functions.
3. Acquire your Tactical Stance allowing Long Gun to hang slung (i.16)
4. Pause for (2) count.
5. Acquire Low Index Ready Position w/F.O.T.G. (i.25a & i.25b)
6. Pause for (2) count.
7. Cognitively think "FIGHT! FIGHT! FIGHT!" while focusing on the Threat.
8. Inhale slowly and deeply, while slowly extending arms to Natural Cradle Rest using toe of Long Gun as a pivot point, while also acquiring proper grip-tension, disengaging the safety mechanism, placing trigger finger on the trigger, keep your weapon level, pivoting weapon up to eye-level and into proper cheek-weld, while pointing it at the Threat while keeping the Threat in focus. DO NOT DEPRESS TRIGGER (i.15 & i.27e)
9. Pause for (2) count.
10. Cognitively think "Assess…Assess…Assess…"
11. Confirm proper Mechanical Alignment (i.1b) If not in Mechanical Alignment, bring weapon into Mechanical Alignment, while cognitively thinking about how your arms and chest feel once in Mechanical Alignment.
12. Memorize the feeling of Mechanical Alignment.
13. Step offline either left or right.
14. Exhale slowly, while relaxing your grip-tension and slowly return to a Low Index Ready Position w/F.O.T.G. (i.25a & i.25b)
15. Perform an After Action Scan, checking to your right and behind, your left and behind. Visually and cognitively identify a specific object in the process i.e. ABCs Training Aides (i.26a, i.26b, i.26c & i.26d)
16. Re-engaging safety mechanism
17. Pause for (2) count.
18. Repeat sequences 1-17 (25) times.

Movement 2 (Low Index Ready)

1. Assure weapon is in Simulated Fire Mode.

2. Perform the following sequences while maintaining complete focus on the Threat and using peripheral vision if needed for the following functions.

3. Acquire your Tactical Stance allowing Long Gun to hang slung (i.16)

4. Pause for (2) count.

5. Acquire Low Index Ready Position w/F.O.T.G. (i.25a & i.25b)

6. Pause for (2) count.

7. Cognitively think "FIGHT! FIGHT! FIGHT!" while focusing on the Threat.

8. Inhale slowly and deeply, while slowly extending arms to Natural Cradle Rest using toe of Long Gun as a pivot point, while also acquiring proper grip-tension, disengaging the safety mechanism, placing trigger finger on the trigger, keep your weapon level, pivoting weapon up to eye-level and into proper cheek-weld, while pointing it at the Threat while keeping the Threat in focus. DO NOT DEPRESS TRIGGER. (i.15 & i.27e)

9. Pause for (2) count.

10. Cognitively think "Assess...Assess...Assess..."

11. Confirm proper Mechanical Alignment (i.1b) If not in Mechanical Alignment, bring weapon into Mechanical Alignment, while cognitively thinking about how your arms and chest feel once in Mechanical Alignment.

12. Memorize the feeling of Mechanical Alignment.

13. Step offline either left or right.

14. Exhale slowly, while relaxing your grip-tension and slowly return to a Low Index Ready Position w/F.O.T.G. (i.25a & i.25b)

15. Perform an After Action Scan, checking to your right and behind, your left and behind. Visually and cognitively identify a specific object in the process i.e. ABCs Training Aides (i.26a, i.26b, i.26c & i.26d)

16. Re-engaging safety mechanism

17. Pause for (2) count.

18. Repeat sequences 1-17 (25) times.

Movement 3 (Low Index Ready)

1. Assure weapon is in Simulated Fire Mode.

2. Perform the following sequences while maintaining complete focus on the Threat and using peripheral vision if needed for the following functions.

3. Acquire your Tactical Stance allowing Long Gun to hang slung (i.16)

4. Pause for (2) count.

5. Acquire Low Index Ready Position w/F.O.T.G. (i.25a & i.25b)

6. Pause for (2) count.
7. Cognitively think "FIGHT! FIGHT! FIGHT!" while focusing on the Threat.
8. Inhale slowly and deeply, while slowly extending arms to Natural Cradle Rest using toe of Long Gun as a pivot point, while also acquiring proper grip-tension, disengaging the safety mechanism, placing your trigger finger on the trigger, keep your weapon level, bringing it up to eye-level, while pointing it at the Threat while keeping the Threat in focus and depressing trigger all the way for a simulated fire upon reaching proper cheek-weld (i.15 & i.27e)
9. Pause for (2) count and follow through.
10. Cognitively think "Assess...Assess...Assess..."
11. Confirm proper Mechanical Alignment (i.1b) If not in Mechanical Alignment, bring weapon into Mechanical Alignment, while cognitively thinking about how your arms and chest feel once in Mechanical Alignment.
12. Memorize the feeling of Mechanical Alignment.
13. Step offline either left or right.
14. Exhale slowly, while relaxing your grip-tension and slowly return to a Low Index Ready Position w/F.O.T.G. (i.25a & i.25b)
15. Perform an After Action Scan, checking to your right and behind, your left and behind. Visually and cognitively identify a specific object in the process i.e. ABCs Training Aides (i.26a, i.26b, i.26c & i.26d)
16. Re-engaging safety mechanism
17. Pause for (2) count.
18. Repeat sequences 1-17 (25) times.

Movement 4 (Low Index Ready)

1. Continually take small steps forward, backward left and right while repeating all sequences of Movements 1-3 (25) times.
2. Repeat all sequences of Movements 1-3 (25) times using a Par-Time Random Beep to initiate simulated fight.
3. Continually take small steps forward, backward left and right while repeating all sequences of Movements 1-3 (25) times using a Par-Time Random Beep to initiate simulated fight.

Sling Carry

Movement 1 (Sling Carry)

1. Assure weapon is in Simulated Fire Mode.
2. Perform the following sequences while maintaining complete focus on the Threat and using peripheral vision if needed for the following functions.
3. Acquire your Tactical Stance allowing Long Gun to hang slung (i.16)
4. Pause for (2) count.
5. Cognitively think "FIGHT! FIGHT! FIGHT!" while focusing on the Threat.
6. Inhale slowly and deeply, while obtaining two handed grip of Long Gun and bringing it to a Low Index Ready Position w/F.O.T.G. (i.25a & i.25b)
7. Slowly extending arms to Natural Cradle Rest using toe of Long Gun as a pivot point, while also acquiring proper grip-tension, disengaging the safety mechanism, placing trigger finger on the trigger, keep your weapon level, pivoting weapon up to eye-level and into proper cheek-weld, while pointing it at the Threat while keeping the Threat in focus. DO NOT DEPRESS TRIGGER (i.15 & i.27e)
8. Pause for (2) count.
9. Cognitively think "Assess...Assess...Assess..."
10. Confirm proper Mechanical Alignment (i.1b) If not in Mechanical Alignment, bring weapon into Mechanical Alignment, while cognitively thinking about how your arms and chest feel once in Mechanical Alignment.
11. Memorize the feeling of Mechanical Alignment.
12. Step offline either left or right.
13. Exhale slowly, while relaxing your grip-tension and slowly return to a Low Index Ready Position w/F.O.T.G. (i.25a & i.25b)
14. Perform an After Action Scan, checking to your right and behind, your left and behind. Visually and cognitively identify a specific object in the process i.e. ABCs Training Aides (i.26a, i.26b, i.26c & i.26d)
15. Re-engaging safety mechanism
16. Pause for (2) count.
17. Repeat sequences 1-16 (25) times.

Movement 2 (Sling Carry)

1. Assure weapon is in Simulated Fire Mode.

2. Perform the following sequences while maintaining complete focus on the Threat and using peripheral vision if needed for the following functions.

3. Acquire your Tactical Stance allowing Long Gun to hang slung (i.16)

4. Pause for (2) count.

5. Cognitively think "FIGHT! FIGHT! FIGHT!" while focusing on the Threat.

6. Inhale slowly and deeply, while obtaining two handed grip of Long Gun and bringing it to a Low Index Ready Position w/F.O.T.G. (i.25a & i.25b)

7. Inhale slowly and deeply, while slowly extending arms to Natural Cradle Rest using toe of Long Gun as a pivot point, while also acquiring proper grip-tension, disengaging the safety mechanism, placing trigger finger on the trigger, keep your weapon level, pivoting weapon up to eye-level and into proper cheek-weld, while pointing it at the Threat while keeping the Threat in focus. DO NOT DEPRESS TRIGGER (i.15 & i.27e)

8. Pause for (2) count.

9. Cognitively think "Assess...Assess...Assess..."

10. Confirm proper Mechanical Alignment (i.1b) If not in Mechanical Alignment, bring weapon into Mechanical Alignment, while cognitively thinking about how your arms and chest feel once in Mechanical Alignment.

11. Memorize the feeling of Mechanical Alignment.

12. Step offline either left or right.

13. Exhale slowly, while relaxing your grip-tension and slowly return to a Low Index Ready Position w/F.O.T.G. (i.25a, i.25b)

14. Perform an After Action Scan, checking to your right and behind, your left and behind. Visually and cognitively identify a specific object in the process i.e. ABCs Training Aides (i.26a, i.26b, i.26c & i.26d)

15. Re-engaging safety mechanism

16. Pause for (2) count.

17. Repeat sequences 1-16 (25) times.

Movement 3 (Sling Carry)

1. Assure weapon is in Simulated Fire Mode.

2. Perform the following sequences while maintaining complete focus on the Threat and using peripheral vision if needed for the following functions.

3. Acquire your Tactical Stance allowing Long Gun to hang slung (i.16)

4. Pause for (2) count.

5. Cognitively think "FIGHT! FIGHT! FIGHT!" while focusing on the Threat.

6. Inhale slowly and deeply, while obtaining two handed grip of Long Gun and bringing it to a Low Index Ready Position w/F.O.T.G. (i.25a & i.25b)

7. Slowly extending arms to Natural Cradle Rest using toe of Long Gun as a pivot point, while also acquiring proper grip-tension, disengaging the safety mechanism, placing your trigger finger on the trigger, keep your weapon level, bringing it up to eye-level, while pointing it at the Threat while keeping the Threat in focus and depressing trigger all the way for a simulated fire upon reaching proper cheek-weld (i.15 & i.27e)

8. Pause for (2) count and follow through.

9. Cognitively think "Assess...Assess...Assess..."

10. Confirm proper Mechanical Alignment (i.1b) If not in Mechanical Alignment, bring weapon into Mechanical Alignment, while cognitively thinking about how your arms and chest feel once in Mechanical Alignment.

11. Memorize the feeling of Mechanical Alignment.

12. Step offline either left or right.

13. Exhale slowly, while relaxing your grip-tension and slowly return to a Low Index Ready Position w/F.O.T.G. (i.25a, i.25b)

14. Perform an After Action Scan, checking to your right and behind, your left and behind. Visually and cognitively identify a specific object in the process i.e. ABCs Training Aides (i.26a, i.26b, i.26c & i.26d)

15. Re-engaging safety mechanism

16. Pause for (2) count.

17. Repeat sequences 1-16 (25) times.

Movement 4 (Sling Carry)

1. Continually take small steps forward, backward left and right while repeating all sequences of Movements 1-3 (25) times.

2. Repeat all sequences of Movements 1-3 (25) times using a Par-Time Random Beep to initiate simulated fight.

3. Continually take small steps forward, backward left and right while repeating all sequences of Movements 1-3 (25) times using a Par-Time Random Beep to initiate simulated fight.

Tactical Reload - Long Gun

Movement 1 (Tactical Reload - Long Gun)

1. Assure weapon is in Simulated Fire Mode.
2. Perform the following sequences while maintaining complete focus on the Threat and using peripheral vision if needed for the following functions.
3. Acquire your Tactical Stance allowing Long Gun to hang slung (i.16)
4. Pause for (2) count.
5. Acquire Low Index Ready Position w/F.O.T.G. (i.25a & i.25b)
6. Pause for (2) count.
7. Inhale slowly and deeply, while slowly extending arms to Natural Cradle Rest using toe of Long Gun as a pivot point, while also acquiring proper grip-tension, disengaging the safety mechanism, placing trigger finger on the trigger, keep your weapon level, pivoting weapon up to eye-level and into proper cheek-weld, while pointing it at the Threat while keeping the Threat in focus. DO NOT DEPRESS TRIGGER (i.15 & i.27e)
8. Pause for (2) count.
9. Cognitively think "TACTICAL LULL" while focusing on the Threat.
10. Pause for (2) count.
11. Cognitively think "RE-CHARGE"
12. Step offline left or right.
13. Bring arms back to Rifle Reload Ready Position w/F.O.T.G. and assessing the chamber then canting it 45° away from ejection port. (i.27a & i.27b)
14. Obtain full fisted grip of simulated partial magazine with Support Hand and remove it from weapon. (i.9)
15. Stow simulated partial magazine and retrieve simulated fresh magazine with full fisted grip. (i.9 & i.27b)
16. Insert simulated fresh magazine (i.27c)
17. Tap the bottom of the weapon and magazine w/palm of Support Hand w/generous force, then tug down on magazine to assure it is properly seated.
18. Regain proper two-handed grip of weapon and return to Low Index Ready Position w/F.O.T.G. (i.25a & i.25b)
19. Pause for (2) count.

20. Perform an After Action Scan, checking to your right and behind, your left and behind. Visually and cognitively identify a specific object in the process i.e. ABCs Training Aides (i.26a, i.26b, i.26c & i.26d)

21. Pause for (2) count.

22. Repeat sequences 1-21 (25) times.

Movement 2 (Tactical Reload -Long Gun)

1. Continually take small steps forward, backward left and right while repeating all sequences of Movements 1-3 (25) times.

2. Repeat all sequences of Movements 1-3 (25) times using a Par-Time Random Beep to initiate simulated fight.

3. Continually take small steps forward, backward left and right while repeating all sequences of Movements 1-3 (25) times using a Par-Time Random Beep to initiate simulated fight.

Combat Reload – Long Gun

Movement 1 (Combat Reload—Long Gun)

1. Stage weapon to create an empty chamber with empty magazine and bolt locked rearward, i.e. no Snap-Caps.

2. Perform the following sequences while maintaining complete focus on the Threat and using peripheral vision if needed for the following functions.

3. Acquire your Tactical Stance allowing Long Gun to hang slung (i.16)

4. Pause for (2) count.

5. Acquire Low Index Ready Position w/F.O.T.G. (i.25a & i.25b)

6. Pause for (2) count.

7. Cognitively think "FIGHT! FIGHT! FIGHT!" while focusing on the Threat.

8. Inhale slowly and deeply, while slowly extending arms to Natural Cradle Rest using toe of Long Gun as a pivot point, while also acquiring proper grip-tension, disengaging the safety mechanism, placing trigger finger on the trigger, keep your weapon level, pivoting weapon up to eye-level and into proper cheek-weld, while pointing it at the Threat while keeping the Threat in focus, fully depressing trigger upon reaching proper cheek-weld. (i.15 & i.27e)

9. Pause for (2) count.

10. WEAPON WON'T FIRE!!!

11. Cognitively think "MALFUNCTION!"

12. Step offline either left or right while slightly canting weapon to briefly assess the ejection port. (i.27a)

13. Visually and cognitively identify an empty weapon.

14. Cognitively think "FEED!"

15. Manipulate magazine release button and quickly flip weapon into Rifle Reload Ready Position w/F.O.T.G. canting it 45° away from ejection port allowing simulated empty magazine to fly free due to centrifugal force. If it doesn't fly free, remove and discard it using Support Hand. (i.27a & i.27b)

16. Retrieve simulated fresh magazine with full fisted grip and load it into weapon. (i.9 & i.27c)

17. Tap the bottom of the weapon and magazine w/palm of Support Hand w/generous force, then tug down on magazine to assure it is properly seated.

18. Bring weapon back to Simulated Fire Mode by pressing the bolt release button or pulling the charge handle. (i.27d)
19. Regain proper two-handed grip of weapon and return to Low Index Ready Position w/F.O.T.G. (i.25a & i.25b)
20. Pause for (2) count.
21. Cognitively think "FIGHT! FIGHT! FIGHT!" while focusing on the Threat.
22. Inhale slowly and deeply, while slowly extending arms to Natural Cradle Rest using toe of Long Gun as a pivot point, while also acquiring proper grip-tension, disengaging the safety mechanism, placing trigger finger on the trigger, keep your weapon level, pivoting weapon up to eye-level and into proper cheek-weld, while pointing it at the Threat while keeping the Threat in focus, fully depressing trigger upon reaching proper cheek-weld. (i.15 & i.27e)
23. Pause for (2) while following through.
24. Cognitively think "Assess...Assess...Assess..."
25. Confirm proper Mechanical Alignment (i.1b) If not in Mechanical Alignment, bring weapon into Mechanical Alignment, while cognitively thinking about how your arms and chest feel once in Mechanical Alignment.
26. Memorize the feeling of Mechanical Alignment.
27. Step offline either left or right.
28. Exhale slowly, while relaxing your grip-tension and slowly return to Low Index Ready Position w/F.O.T.G. (i.25a & i.25b)
29. Perform an After Action Scan, checking to your right and behind, your left and behind. Visually and cognitively identify a specific object in the process i.e. ABCs Training Aides (i.26a, i.26b, i.26c & i.26d)
30. Pause for (2) count.
31. Re-engage the safety mechanism.
32. Pause for (2) count.
33. Re-stage weapon to create an empty chamber with empty magazine and bolt locked rearward, i.e. no Snap-Caps.
34. Repeat sequences 1-33 (25) times.

Movement 2 (Combat Reload -Long Gun)

1. Continually take small steps forward, backward left and right while repeating all sequences of Movements 1-3 (25) times.
2. Repeat all sequences of Movements 1-3 (25) times using a Par-Time Random Beep to initiate simulated fight.

3. Continually take small steps forward, backward left and right while repeating all sequences of Movements 1-3 (25) times using a Par-Time Random Beep to initiate simulated fight.

Type 1 Malfunction - Long Gun

Movement 1 (Type 1 Malfunction—Long Gun)

1. Stage weapon to create an empty chamber with bolt locked forward and a simulated full magazine w/ Snap-Caps.
2. Perform the following sequences while maintaining complete focus on the Threat and using peripheral vision if needed for the following functions.
3. Acquire your Tactical Stance allowing Long Gun to hang slung (i.16)
4. Pause for (2) count.
5. Acquire Low Index Ready Position w/F.O.T.G. (i.25a & i.25b)
6. Pause for (2) count.
7. Cognitively think "FIGHT! FIGHT! FIGHT!" while focusing on the Threat.
8. Inhale slowly and deeply, while slowly extending arms to Natural Cradle Rest using toe of Long Gun as a pivot point, while also acquiring proper grip-tension, disengaging the safety mechanism, placing trigger finger on the trigger, keep your weapon level, pivoting weapon up to eye-level and into proper cheek-weld, while pointing it at the Threat while keeping the Threat in focus, fully depressing trigger upon reaching proper cheek-weld. (i.15 & i.27e)
9. Pause for (2) count.
10. WEAPON WON'T FIRE!!!
11. Cognitively think "MALFUNCTION!"
12. Step offline either left or right while slightly canting weapon to briefly assess the ejection port. (i.27a)
13. Visually and cognitively identify a Type 1 Malfunction.
14. Cognitively think "TAP - RACK - REENGAGE"
15. Tap the bottom of the weapon and magazine w/palm of Support Hand w/generous force, then tug down on magazine to assure it is properly seated.
16. Bring weapon back to Simulated Fire Mode by pressing the bolt release button or pulling the charge handle. (i.27d)
17. Regain proper two-handed grip of weapon and return to Low Index Ready Position w/F.O.T.G. (i.25a & i.25b)
18. Pause for (2) count.
19. Cognitively think "FIGHT! FIGHT! FIGHT!" while focusing on the Threat.

20. Inhale slowly and deeply, while slowly extending arms to Natural Cradle Rest using toe of Long Gun as a pivot point, while also acquiring proper grip-tension, disengaging the safety mechanism, placing trigger finger on the trigger, keep your weapon level, pivoting weapon up to eye-level and into proper cheek-weld, while pointing it at the Threat while keeping the Threat in focus, fully depressing trigger upon reaching proper cheek-weld. (i.15 & i.27e)

21. Pause for (2) while following through.

22. Cognitively think "Assess...Assess...Assess..."

23. Confirm proper Mechanical Alignment (i.1b) If not in Mechanical Alignment, bring weapon into Mechanical Alignment, while cognitively thinking about how your arms and chest feel once in Mechanical Alignment.

24. Memorize the feeling of Mechanical Alignment.

25. Step offline either left or right.

26. Exhale slowly, while relaxing your grip-tension and slowly return to Low Index Ready Position w/F.O.T.G. (i.25a & i.25b)

27. Perform an After Action Scan, checking to your right and behind, your left and behind. Visually and cognitively identify a specific object in the process i.e. ABCs Training Aides (i.26a, i.26b, i.26c & i.26d)

28. Pause for (2) count.

29. Re-engage the safety mechanism.

30. Pause for (2) count.

31. Re-stage weapon to create an empty chamber with bolt locked forward and a simulated full magazine w/ Snap-Caps.

32. Repeat sequences 1-31 (25) times.

Movement 2 (Type 1 Malfunction—Long Gun)

1. Continually take small steps forward, backward left and right while repeating all sequences of Movements 1-3 (25) times.

2. Repeat all sequences of Movements 1-3 (25) times using a Par-Time Random Beep to initiate simulated fight.

3. Continually take small steps forward, backward left and right while repeating all sequences of Movements 1-3 (25) times using a Par-Time Random Beep to initiate simulated fight.

Type 2 Malfunction - Long Gun

Movement 1 (Type 2 Malfunction—Long Gun)

1. Stage weapon to create an empty chamber, simulated full magazine and a Type 2 Stovepipe w/ Snap-Caps.
2. Perform the following sequences while maintaining complete focus on the Threat and using peripheral vision if needed for the following functions.
3. Acquire your Tactical Stance allowing Long Gun to hang slung (i.16)
4. Pause for (2) count.
5. Acquire Low Index Ready Position w/F.O.T.G. (i.25a & i.25b)
6. Pause for (2) count.
7. Cognitively think "FIGHT! FIGHT! FIGHT!" while focusing on the Threat.
8. Inhale slowly and deeply, while slowly extending arms to Natural Cradle Rest using toe of Long Gun as a pivot point, while also acquiring proper grip-tension, disengaging the safety mechanism, placing trigger finger on the trigger, keep your weapon level, pivoting weapon up to eye-level and into proper cheek-weld, while pointing it at the Threat while keeping the Threat in focus, fully depressing trigger upon reaching proper cheek-weld. (i.15 & i.27e)
9. Pause for (2) count.
10. WEAPON WON'T FIRE!!!
11. Cognitively think "MALFUNCTION!"
12. Step offline either left or right while slightly canting weapon to briefly assess the ejection port. (i.27a)
13. Visually and cognitively identify a Type 2 Malfunction.
14. Cognitively think "TAP - SWEEP - RACK - REENGAGE"
15. Tap the bottom of the weapon and magazine w/palm of Support Hand w/generous force, then tug down on magazine to assure it is properly seated.
16. Cant weapon in a manner that allows ease of access for an overhand sweep of the stovepiped casing with your Support Hand.
17. Bring weapon back to Simulated Fire Mode by pulling and releasing the charge handle.
18. Regain proper two-handed grip of weapon and return to Low Index Ready Position w/F.O.T.G. (i.25a & i.25b)
19. Pause for (2) count.

20. Cognitively think "FIGHT! FIGHT! FIGHT!" while focusing on the Threat.

21. Inhale slowly and deeply, while slowly extending arms to Natural Cradle Rest using toe of Long Gun as a pivot point, while also acquiring proper grip-tension, disengaging the safety mechanism, placing trigger finger on the trigger, keep your weapon level, pivoting weapon up to eye-level and into proper cheek-weld, while pointing it at the Threat while keeping the Threat in focus, fully depressing trigger upon reaching proper cheek-weld. (i.15 & i.27e)

22. Pause for (2) while following through.

23. Cognitively think "Assess...Assess...Assess..."

24. Confirm proper Mechanical Alignment (i.1b) If not in Mechanical Alignment, bring weapon into Mechanical Alignment, while cognitively thinking about how your arms and chest feel once in Mechanical Alignment.

25. Memorize the feeling of Mechanical Alignment.

26. Step offline either left or right.

27. Exhale slowly, while relaxing your grip-tension and slowly return to Low Index Ready Position w/F.O.T.G. (i.25a & i.25b)

28. Perform an After Action Scan, checking to your right and behind, your left and behind. Visually and cognitively identify a specific object in the process i.e. ABCs Training Aides (i.26a, i.26b, i.26c & i.26d)

29. Pause for (2) count.

30. Re-engage the safety mechanism.

31. Pause for (2) count.

32. Re-stage weapon to create an empty chamber, simulated full magazine and a Type 2 Stovepipe w/ Snap-Caps.

33. Repeat sequences 1-32 (25) times.

Movement 2 (Type 2 Malfunction—Long Gun)

1. Continually take small steps forward, backward left and right while repeating all sequences of Movements 1-3 (25) times.

2. Repeat all sequences of Movements 1-3 (25) times using a Par-Time Random Beep to initiate simulated fight.

3. Continually take small steps forward, backward left and right while repeating all sequences of Movements 1-3 (25) times using a Par-Time Random Beep to initiate simulated fight.

Type 3 Malfunction – Long Gun

Movement 1 (Type 3 Malfunction—Long Gun)

1. Stage weapon to create a Type 3 Double-Feed w/ Snap-Caps and a simulated full magazine. (i.14a & i.14b)
2. Perform the following sequences while maintaining complete focus on the Threat and using peripheral vision if needed for the following functions.
3. Acquire your Tactical Stance. (i.16)
4. Pause for (2) count.
5. Cognitively think "FIGHT! FIGHT! FIGHT!" while focusing on the Threat.
6. Inhale slowly and deeply, while slowly extending arms to Natural Arm Extension, while also acquiring proper grip-tension, disengaging the safety mechanism, placing your trigger finger on the trigger, keep your weapon level, bringing it up to eye-level, while pointing it at the Threat while keeping the Threat in focus and depressing trigger all the way for a simulated fire upon reaching Natural Arm Extension (i.7a, i.7b & i.1b)
7. WEAPON WON'T FIRE!!!
8. Cognitively think "MALFUNCTION!"
9. Step offline either left or right while slightly canting weapon to briefly assess the ejection port.
10. Visually and cognitively identify a Type 3 Malfunction.
11. Cognitively think "STRIP - RACK - FEED - TAP - RACK - REENGAGE"
12. Manipulate magazine release button and quickly flip weapon into Rifle Reload Ready Position w/F.O.T.G. canting it 45° away from ejection port allowing simulated empty magazine to fly free due to centrifugal force. If it doesn't fly free, remove and discard it using Support Hand. (i.27a & i.27b)
13. Rack the action (3) times to assure the malfunction clears.
14. Retrieve simulated fresh magazine with full fisted grip and load it into weapon. (i.9 & i.27c)
15. Tap the bottom of the weapon and magazine w/palm of Support Hand w/generous force, then tug down on magazine to assure it is properly seated.
16. Bring weapon back to Simulated Fire Mode by pressing the bolt release button or pulling the charge handle. (i.27d)

17. Regain proper two-handed grip of weapon and return to Low Index Ready Position w/F.O.T.G. (i.25a & i.25b)
18. Pause for (2) count.
19. Cognitively think "FIGHT! FIGHT! FIGHT!" while focusing on the Threat.
20. Inhale slowly and deeply, while slowly extending arms to Natural Cradle Rest using toe of Long Gun as a pivot point, while also acquiring proper grip-tension, disengaging the safety mechanism, placing trigger finger on the trigger, keep your weapon level, pivoting weapon up to eye-level and into proper cheek-weld, while pointing it at the Threat while keeping the Threat in focus, fully depressing trigger upon reaching proper cheek-weld. (i.15 & i.27e)
21. Pause for (2) while following through.
22. Cognitively think "Assess...Assess...Assess..."
23. Confirm proper Mechanical Alignment (i.1b) If not in Mechanical Alignment, bring weapon into Mechanical Alignment, while cognitively thinking about how your arms and chest feel once in Mechanical Alignment.
24. Memorize the feeling of Mechanical Alignment.
25. Step offline either left or right.
26. Exhale slowly, while relaxing your grip-tension and slowly return to Low Index Ready Position w/F.O.T.G. (i.25a & i.25b)
27. Perform an After Action Scan, checking to your right and behind, your left and behind. Visually and cognitively identify a specific object in the process i.e. ABCs Training Aides (i.26a, i.26b, i.26c & i.26d)
28. Pause for (2) count.
29. Re-engage the safety mechanism.
30. Pause for (2) count.
31. Re-stage weapon to create an empty chamber with empty magazine and bolt locked rearward, i.e. no Snap-Caps.
32. Repeat sequences 1-31 (25) times.

Movement 2 (Type 3 Malfunction—Long Gun)

1. Continually take small steps forward, backward left and right while repeating all sequences of Movements 1-3 (25) times.
2. Repeat all sequences of Movements 1-3 (25) times using a Par-Time Random Beep to initiate simulated fight.
3. Continually take small steps forward, backward left and right while repeating all sequences of Movements 1-3 (25) times using a Par-Time Random Beep to initiate simulated fight.

DECREASING PAR-TIME DRILLS LONG GUN

These drills are best accomplished using a shooting par-timer

Index Ready (Par-Time Speed)

Movement 1

Assure weapon is in Simulated Fire Mode and perform the following steps while maintaining complete focus on the Threat and using peripheral vision if needed for the following functions.

1. Acquire Index Ready Position w/F.O.T.G. and wait for beep.

START BEEP...

2. Cognitively think "FIGHT! FIGHT! FIGHT!" while focusing on the Threat, inhale slowly and deeply, while slowly extending arms to Natural Cradle Rest using toe of Long Gun as a pivot point, while also acquiring proper grip-tension, disengaging the safety mechanism, placing your trigger finger on the trigger, keep your weapon level, bringing it up to eye-level, while pointing it at the Threat while keeping the Threat in focus and depressing trigger all the way for a simulated fire upon reaching proper cheek-weld

END BEEP...

3. Pause for (2) while following through, cognitively think "Assess...Assess...Assess..."
4. Confirm proper Mechanical Alignment. If not in Mechanical Alignment, bring weapon into Mechanical Alignment, while cognitively thinking about how your arms and chest feel once in Mechanical Alignment.
5. Memorize the feeling of Mechanical Alignment.
6. Step offline either left or right, exhale slowly, while relaxing your grip-tension and slowly return to an Index Ready Position w/F.O.T.G. perform an After Action Scan, checking to your right and behind, your left and behind. Visually and cognitively identify a specific object in the process i.e. ABCs Training Aides.
7. Pause for (2) count.
8. Return to Simulated Fire Mode.
9. Re-engage the safety mechanism.
10. Pause for (2) count.
11. Repeat sequences 1-10 (25) times.

Movement 2

1. Reset Par-Timer and Repeat (25) Times with-in 2 seconds.

Movement 3

1. Reset Par-Timer and Repeat (25) Times with-in 1.5 seconds.

Movement 4

    1. Reset Par-Timer and Repeat (25) Times with-in 1.3 seconds.

Movement 5

    1. Reset Par-Timer and Repeat (25) Times with-in 0.9 seconds.

Movement 6

    1. Reset Par-Timer and repeat (25) Times with-in 0.8 seconds.

Movement 7

    1. Reset Par-Timer, continually take small steps forward, backward left, right and repeat Movements 1-6 (25) times.

Low Index Ready
(Par-Time Speed)

Movement 1

Assure weapon is in Simulated Fire Mode and perform the following steps while maintaining complete focus on the Threat and using peripheral vision if needed for the following functions.

1. Acquire Low Index Ready Position w/F.O.T.G. and wait for beep

START BEEP...

2. Cognitively think "FIGHT! FIGHT! FIGHT!" while focusing on the Threat, inhale slowly and deeply, while slowly extending arms to Natural Cradle Rest using toe of Long Gun as a pivot point, while also acquiring proper grip-tension, disengaging the safety mechanism, placing your trigger finger on the trigger, keep your weapon level, bringing it up to eye-level, while pointing it at the Threat while keeping the Threat in focus and depressing trigger all the way for a simulated fire upon reaching proper cheek-weld

END BEEP...

3. Pause for (2) while following through, cognitively think "Assess...Assess...Assess..."
4. Confirm proper Mechanical Alignment. If not in Mechanical Alignment, bring weapon into Mechanical Alignment, while cognitively thinking about how your arms and chest feel once in Mechanical Alignment.
5. Memorize the feeling of Mechanical Alignment.
6. Step offline either left or right, exhale slowly, while relaxing your grip-tension and slowly return to a Low Index Ready Position w/F.O.T.G. perform an After Action Scan, checking to your right and behind, your left and behind. Visually and cognitively identify a specific object in the process i.e. ABCs Training Aides.
7. Pause for (2) count.
8. Return to Simulated Fire Mode.
9. Re-engage the safety mechanism.
10. Pause for (2) count.
11. Repeat sequences 1-10 (25) times.

Movement 2

1. Reset Par-Timer and Repeat (25) Times with-in 2 seconds.

Movement 3

    1. Reset Par-Timer and Repeat (25) Times with-in 1.5 seconds.

Movement 4

    1. Reset Par-Timer and Repeat (25) Times with-in 1.3 seconds.

Movement 5

    1. Reset Par-Timer and Repeat (25) Times with-in 0.9 seconds.

Movement 6

    1. Reset Par-Timer and repeat (25) Times with-in 0.8 seconds.

Movement 7

    1. Reset Par-Timer, continually take small steps forward, backward left, right and repeat Movements 1-6 (25) times.

Sling Carry
(Par-Time Speed)

Movement 1

Assure weapon is in Simulated Fire Mode and perform the following steps while maintaining complete focus on the Threat and using peripheral vision if needed for the following functions.

1. Acquire your Tactical Stance allowing Long Gun to hang slung and wait for beep.

START BEEP...

2. Cognitively think "FIGHT! FIGHT! FIGHT!" while focusing on the Threat, inhale slowly and deeply, while obtaining two handed grip of Long Gun and bring it to a Low Index Ready Position w/F.O.T.G. while slowly extending arms to Natural Cradle Rest using toe of Long Gun as a pivot point, while also acquiring proper grip-tension, disengaging the safety mechanism, placing your trigger finger on the trigger, keep your weapon level, bringing it up to eye-level, while pointing it at the Threat while keeping the Threat in focus and depressing trigger all the way for a simulated fire upon reaching proper cheek-weld

END BEEP...

3. Pause for (2) while following through, cognitively think "Assess...Assess...Assess..."

4. Confirm proper Mechanical Alignment. If not in Mechanical Alignment, bring weapon into Mechanical Alignment, while cognitively thinking about how your arms and chest feel once in Mechanical Alignment.

5. Memorize the feeling of Mechanical Alignment.

6. Step offline either left or right, exhale slowly, while relaxing your grip-tension and slowly return to a Low Index Ready Position w/F.O.T.G. perform an After Action Scan, checking to your right and behind, your left and behind. Visually and cognitively identify a specific object in the process i.e. ABCs Training Aides.

7. Pause for (2) count.

8. Return to Simulated Fire Mode.

9. Re-engage the safety mechanism.

10. Pause for (2) count.

11. Repeat sequences 1-10 (25) times.

Movement 2

    1. Reset Par-Timer and Repeat (25) Times with-in 2 seconds.

Movement 3

    1. Reset Par-Timer and Repeat (25) Times with-in 1.5 seconds.

Movement 4

    1. Reset Par-Timer and Repeat (25) Times with-in 1.3 seconds.

Movement 5

    1. Reset Par-Timer and Repeat (25) Times with-in 0.9 seconds.

Movement 6

    1. Reset Par-Timer and repeat (25) Times with-in 0.8 seconds.

Movement 7

    1. Reset Par-Timer, continually take small steps forward, backward left, right and repeat Movements 1-6 (25) times.

Tactical Reload –Long Gun
(Par-Time Speed)

Movement 1

Assure weapon is in Simulated Fire Mode and perform the following steps while maintaining complete focus on the Threat and using peripheral vision if needed for the following functions.

1. Acquire your Tactical Stance with arms extended to Natural Cradle Ready and proper cheek-weld with trigger finger on the trigger and pointing weapon at the Threat while wait for beep.

START BEEP...

2. Cognitively think "TACTICAL LULL" while focusing on the Threat, then cognitively think "RE-CHARGE", stepping offline left or right, bringing arms back to Rifle Reload Ready Position w/F.O.T.G. and weapon canted 45° towards ejection port, remove simulated partial magazine with full fisted grip with Support Hand, retain and stow simulated partial magazine and retrieve and load simulated fresh magazine, tap the bottom of the weapon and mag-well w/palm of Support Hand w/generous force, regain two-handed grip of weapon and return to Low Index Ready Position w/F.O.T.G.

END BEEP...

3. Pause for (2) while cognitively think "Assess...Assess...Assess..."
4. Step offline either left or right, exhale slowly, perform an After Action Scan, checking to your right and behind, your left and behind. Visually and cognitively identify a specific object in the process i.e. ABCs Training Aides.
5. Pause for (2) count.
6. Re-engage the safety mechanism.
7. Repeat sequences 1-6 (25) times.

Movement 2

1. Reset Par-Timer and Repeat (25) Times with-in 2 seconds.

Movement 3

1. Reset Par-Timer and Repeat (25) Times with-in 1.5 seconds.

Movement 4

1. Reset Par-Timer and Repeat (25) Times with-in 1.3 seconds.

Movement 5

1. Reset Par-Timer and Repeat (25) Times with-in 0.9 seconds.

Movement 6

1. Reset Par-Timer and repeat (25) Times with-in 0.8 seconds.

Movement 7

1. Reset Par-Timer, continually take small steps forward, backward left, right and repeat Movements 1-6 (25) times.

Combat Reload – Long Gun
(Par-Time Speed)

Movement 1

Assure weapon is staged to create an empty chamber with empty magazine and action locked to the rear, i.e. no Snap-Caps and perform the following steps while maintaining complete focus on the Threat and using peripheral vision if needed for the following functions.

1. Acquire your Tactical Stance with arms extended to Natural Cradle Ready and proper cheek-weld with trigger finger on the trigger and pointing weapon at the Threat while wait for beep.

START BEEP...

2. Cognitively think "FIGHT! FIGHT! FIGHT!" while focusing on the Threat, inhale slowly and deeply, while slowly extending arms to Natural Cradle Rest using toe of Long Gun as a pivot point, while also acquiring proper grip-tension, disengaging the safety mechanism, placing trigger finger on the trigger, keep your weapon level, pivoting weapon up to eye-level and into proper cheek-weld, while pointing it at the Threat while keeping the Threat in focus, fully depressing trigger upon reaching proper cheek-weld, WEAPON WON'T FIRE!!! cognitively think "MALFUNCTION!" step offline either left or right while slightly canting weapon to briefly assess the ejection port, visually and cognitively identify an empty weapon, cognitively think "FEED!" manipulate magazine release button and quickly flip weapon into Rifle Reload Ready Position w/F.O.T.G. canting it 45° away from ejection port allowing simulated empty magazine to fly free due to centrifugal force. If it doesn't fly free, remove and discard it using Support Hand, retrieve simulated fresh magazine with full fisted grip and load it into weapon, tap the bottom of the weapon and magazine w/palm of Support Hand w/generous force, then tug down on magazine to assure it is properly seated, bring weapon back to Simulated Fire Mode by pressing the bolt release button or pulling the charge handle, regain proper two-handed grip of weapon and return to Low Index Ready Position w/F.O.T.G. cognitively think "FIGHT! FIGHT! FIGHT!" while focusing on the Threat, Inhale slowly and deeply, while slowly extending arms to Natural Cradle Rest using toe of Long Gun as a pivot point, while also acquiring proper grip-tension, disengaging the safety mechanism, placing trigger finger on the trigger, keep your weapon level, pivoting weapon up to eye-level and into proper cheek-weld, while pointing it at the Threat while keeping the Threat in focus, fully depressing trigger upon reaching proper cheek-weld

END BEEP...

3. Pause for (2) following through while cognitively think "Assess...Assess...Assess..."
4. Confirm proper Mechanical Alignment. If not in Mechanical Alignment, bring weapon into Mechanical Alignment, while cognitively thinking about how your arms and chest feel once in Mechanical Alignment.
5. Memorize the feeling of Mechanical Alignment.
6. Return to Low Index Ready Position w/F.O.T.G.
7. Step offline either left or right, exhale slowly, while relaxing your grip-tension and slowly return to an Index Ready Position w/F.O.T.G. perform an After Action Scan, checking to your right and behind, your left and behind. Visually and cognitively identify a specific object in the process i.e. ABCs Training Aides.
8. Pause for (2) count.
9. Re-engage the safety mechanism.
10. Pause for (2) count.
11. Repeat sequences 1-10 (25) times.

Movement 2

1. Reset Par-Timer and Repeat (25) Times with-in 2 seconds.

Movement 3

1. Reset Par-Timer and Repeat (25) Times with-in 1.5 seconds.

Movement 4

1. Reset Par-Timer and Repeat (25) Times with-in 1.3 seconds.

Movement 5

1. Reset Par-Timer and Repeat (25) Times with-in 0.9 seconds.

Movement 6

1. Reset Par-Timer and repeat (25) Times with-in 0.8 seconds.

Movement 7

1. Reset Par-Timer, continually take small steps forward, backward left, right and repeat Movements 1-6 (25) times.

Type 1 Malfunction-Long Gun
(Par-Time Speed)

Movement 1

Assure weapon is staged to create an empty chamber with bolt locked forward and a simulated full magazine w/ Snap-Caps and perform the following steps while maintaining complete focus on the Threat and using peripheral vision if needed for the following functions.

1. Acquire your Tactical Stance with arms extended to Natural Cradle Ready and proper cheek-weld with trigger finger on the trigger and pointing weapon at the Threat while wait for beep.

START BEEP...

2. Cognitively think "FIGHT! FIGHT! FIGHT!" while focusing on the Threat, inhale slowly and deeply, while slowly extending arms to Natural Cradle Rest using toe of Long Gun as a pivot point, while also acquiring proper grip-tension, disengaging the safety mechanism, placing trigger finger on the trigger, keep your weapon level, pivoting weapon up to eye-level and into proper cheek-weld, while pointing it at the Threat while keeping the Threat in focus, fully depressing trigger upon reaching proper cheek-weld, WEAPON WON'T FIRE!!! then Cognitively think "MALFUNCTION! "step offline either left or right while slightly canting weapon to briefly assess the ejection port, visually and cognitively identify a Type 1 Malfunction, cognitively think "TAP - RACK - REENGAGE" tap the bottom of the weapon and magazine w/palm of Support Hand w/generous force, then tug down on magazine to assure it is properly seated, bring weapon back to Simulated Fire Mode by pressing the bolt release button or pulling the charge handle, regain proper two-handed grip of weapon and return to Low Index Ready Position w/F.O.T.G. cognitively think "FIGHT! FIGHT! FIGHT!" while focusing on the Threat, Inhale slowly and deeply, while slowly extending arms to Natural Cradle Rest using toe of Long Gun as a pivot point, while also acquiring proper grip-tension, disengaging the safety mechanism, placing trigger finger on the trigger, keep your weapon level, pivoting weapon up to eye-level and into proper cheek-weld, while pointing it at the Threat while keeping the Threat in focus, fully depressing trigger upon reaching proper cheek-weld

END BEEP...

3. Pause for (2) following through while cognitively think "Assess...Assess...Assess..."

4. Confirm proper Mechanical Alignment. If not in Mechanical Alignment, bring weapon into Mechanical Alignment, while cognitively thinking about how your arms and chest feel once in Mechanical Alignment.
5. Memorize the feeling of Mechanical Alignment.
6. Return to Low Index Ready Position w/F.O.T.G.
7. Step offline either left or right, exhale slowly, while relaxing your grip-tension and slowly return to an Index Ready Position w/F.O.T.G. perform an After Action Scan, checking to your right and behind, your left and behind. Visually and cognitively identify a specific object in the process i.e. ABCs Training Aides.
8. Pause for (2) count.
9. Re-engage the safety mechanism.
10. Pause for (2) count.
11. Repeat sequences 1-10 (25) times.

Movement 2

1. Reset Par-Timer and Repeat (25) Times with-in 2 seconds.

Movement 3

1. Reset Par-Timer and Repeat (25) Times with-in 1.5 seconds.

Movement 4

1. Reset Par-Timer and Repeat (25) Times with-in 1.3 seconds.

Movement 5

1. Reset Par-Timer and Repeat (25) Times with-in 0.9 seconds.

Movement 6

1. Reset Par-Timer and repeat (25) Times with-in 0.8 seconds.

Movement 7

1. Reset Par-Timer, continually take small steps forward, backward left, right and repeat Movements 1-6 (25) times.

Type 2 Malfunction - Long Gun
(Par-Time Speed)

Movement 1

Assure weapon is staged to create an empty chamber with bolt locked forward and a simulated full magazine w/ Snap-Caps and perform the following steps while maintaining complete focus on the Threat and using peripheral vision if needed for the following functions.

1. Acquire your Tactical Stance with arms extended to Natural Cradle Ready and proper cheek-weld with trigger finger on the trigger and pointing weapon at the Threat while wait for beep.

START BEEP...

2. Cognitively think "FIGHT! FIGHT! FIGHT!" while focusing on the Threat, inhale slowly and deeply, while slowly extending arms to Natural Cradle Rest using toe of Long Gun as a pivot point, while also acquiring proper grip-tension, disengaging the safety mechanism, placing trigger finger on the trigger, keep your weapon level, pivoting weapon up to eye-level and into proper cheek-weld, while pointing it at the Threat while keeping the Threat in focus, fully depressing trigger upon reaching proper cheek-weld, WEAPON WON'T FIRE!!! then Cognitively think "MALFUNCTION!" step offline either left or right while slightly canting weapon to briefly assess the ejection port, visually and cognitively identify a Type 2 Malfunction, cognitively think "TAP - SWEEP - RACK - REENGAGE" tap the bottom of the weapon and magazine w/palm of Support Hand w/generous force, then tug down on magazine to assure it is properly seated, cant weapon in a manner that allows ease of access for an overhand sweep of the stovepiped casing with your Support Hand, bring weapon back to Simulated Fire Mode by pressing the bolt release button or pulling the charge handle, regain proper two-handed grip of weapon and return to Low Index Ready Position w/F.O.T.G. cognitively think "FIGHT! FIGHT! FIGHT!" while focusing on the Threat, Inhale slowly and deeply, while slowly extending arms to Natural Cradle Rest using toe of Long Gun as a pivot point, while also acquiring proper grip-tension, disengaging the safety mechanism, placing trigger finger on the trigger, keep your weapon level, pivoting weapon up to eye-level and into proper cheek-weld, while pointing it at the Threat while keeping the Threat in focus, fully depressing trigger upon reaching proper cheek-weld

END BEEP...

3. Pause for (2) following through while cognitively think "Assess...Assess...Assess..."

4. Confirm proper Mechanical Alignment. If not in Mechanical Alignment, bring weapon into Mechanical Alignment, while cognitively thinking about how your arms and chest feel once in Mechanical Alignment.
5. Memorize the feeling of Mechanical Alignment.
6. Return to Low Index Ready Position w/F.O.T.G.
7. Step offline either left or right, exhale slowly, while relaxing your grip-tension and slowly return to an Index Ready Position w/F.O.T.G. perform an After Action Scan, checking to your right and behind, your left and behind. Visually and cognitively identify a specific object in the process i.e. ABCs Training Aides.
8. Pause for (2) count.
9. Re-engage the safety mechanism.
10. Pause for (2) count.
11. Repeat sequences 1-10 (25) times.

Movement 2

1. Reset Par-Timer and Repeat (25) Times with-in 2 seconds.

Movement 3

1. Reset Par-Timer and Repeat (25) Times with-in 1.5 seconds.

Movement 4

1. Reset Par-Timer and Repeat (25) Times with-in 1.3 seconds.

Movement 5

1. Reset Par-Timer and Repeat (25) Times with-in 0.9 seconds.

Movement 6

1. Reset Par-Timer and repeat (25) Times with-in 0.8 seconds.

Movement 7

1. Reset Par-Timer, continually take small steps forward, backward left, right and repeat Movements 1-6 (25) times.

Type 3 Malfunction – Long Gun
(Par-Time Speed)

Movement 1

Assure weapon is staged to create a Type 3 Malfunction Double-Feed w/ Snap-Caps and a simulated full magazine and perform the following steps while maintaining complete focus on the Threat and using peripheral vision if needed for the following functions.

1. Acquire your Tactical Stance with arms extended to Natural Cradle Ready and proper cheek-weld with trigger finger on the trigger and pointing weapon at the Threat while wait for beep.

START BEEP...

2. Cognitively think "FIGHT! FIGHT! FIGHT!" while focusing on the Threat, inhale slowly and deeply, while slowly extending arms to Natural Cradle Rest using toe of Long Gun as a pivot point, while also acquiring proper grip-tension, disengaging the safety mechanism, placing trigger finger on the trigger, keep your weapon level, pivoting weapon up to eye-level and into proper cheek-weld, while pointing it at the Threat while keeping the Threat in focus, fully depressing trigger upon reaching proper cheek-weld, WEAPON WON'T FIRE!!! then Cognitively think "MALFUNCTION!" step offline either left or right while slightly canting weapon to briefly assess the ejection port, visually and cognitively identify a Type 3 Malfunction, cognitively think "STRIP - RACK - FEED - TAP - RACK - REENGAGE" manipulate magazine release button and quickly flip weapon into Rifle Reload Ready Position w/F.O.T.G. canting it 45° away from ejection port allowing simulated empty magazine to fly free due to centrifugal force. If it doesn't fly free, remove and discard it using Support Hand, rack the action (3) times to assure the malfunction clears, retrieve simulated fresh magazine with full fisted grip and load it into weapon, tap the bottom of the weapon and magazine w/palm of Support Hand w/generous force, then tug down on magazine to assure it is properly seated, bring weapon back to Simulated Fire Mode by pressing the bolt release button or pulling the charge handle, regain proper two-handed grip of weapon and return to Low Index Ready Position w/F.O.T.G. cognitively think "FIGHT! FIGHT! FIGHT!" while focusing on the Threat, Inhale slowly and deeply, while slowly extending arms to Natural Cradle Rest using toe of Long Gun as a pivot point, while also acquiring proper grip-tension, disengaging the safety mechanism, placing trigger finger on the trigger, keep your weapon level, pivoting weapon up to eye-level and into proper cheek-weld, while pointing it at the Threat while keeping the Threat in focus, fully depressing trigger upon reaching proper cheek-weld

END BEEP...

3. Pause for (2) following through while cognitively think "Assess...Assess...Assess..."
4. Confirm proper Mechanical Alignment. If not in Mechanical Alignment, bring weapon into Mechanical Alignment, while cognitively thinking about how your arms and chest feel once in Mechanical Alignment.
5. Memorize the feeling of Mechanical Alignment.
6. Return to Low Index Ready Position w/F.O.T.G.
7. Step offline either left or right, exhale slowly, while relaxing your grip-tension and slowly return to an Index Ready Position w/F.O.T.G. perform an After Action Scan, checking to your right and behind, your left and behind. Visually and cognitively identify a specific object in the process i.e. ABCs Training Aides.
8. Pause for (2) count.
9. Re-engage the safety mechanism.
10. Pause for (2) count.
11. Repeat sequences 1-10 (25) times.

Movement 2

1. Reset Par-Timer and Repeat (25) Times with-in 2 seconds.

Movement 3

1. Reset Par-Timer and Repeat (25) Times with-in 1.5 seconds.

Movement 4

1. Reset Par-Timer and Repeat (25) Times with-in 1.3 seconds.

Movement 5

1. Reset Par-Timer and Repeat (25) Times with-in 0.9 seconds.

Movement 6

1. Reset Par-Timer and repeat (25) Times with-in 0.8 seconds.

Movement 7

1. Reset Par-Timer, continually take small steps forward, backward left, right and repeat Movements 1-6 (25) times.

IMAGES

i.1a

NOTE: Handgun Iron Sights

i.1b

NOTE: Rifle Iron Sights

i.2a

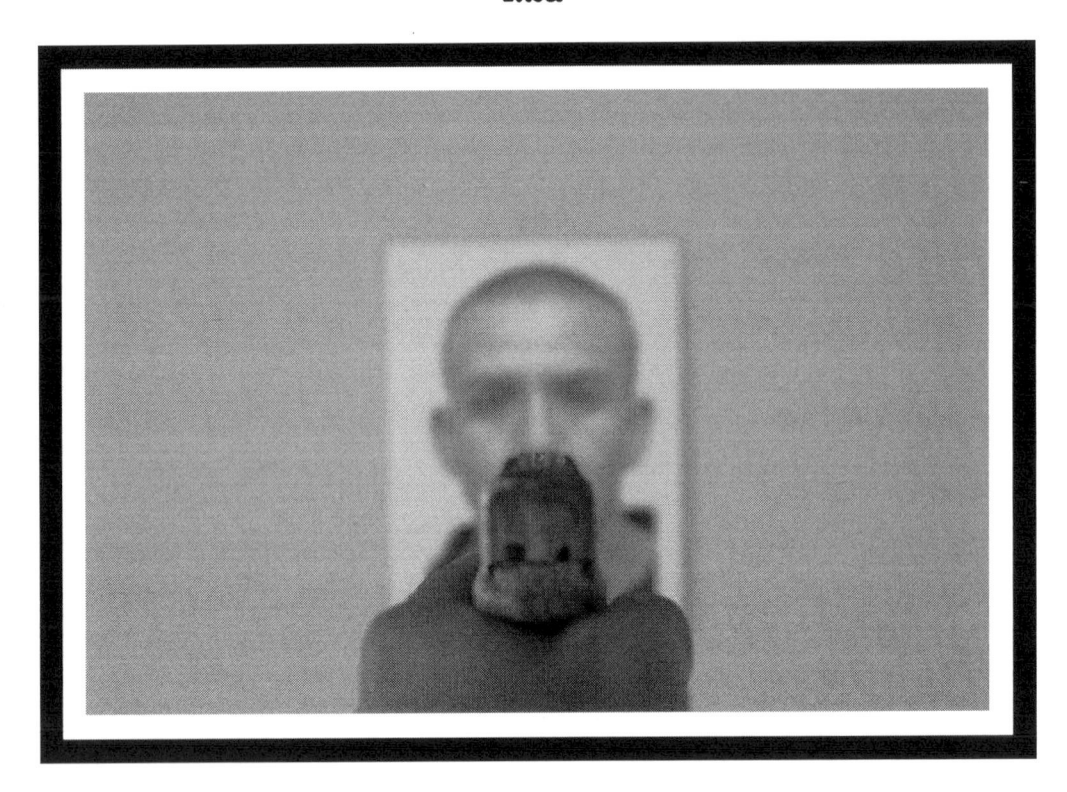

NOTE: Traditional Sight Picture. Sights in focus while threat is out of focus.

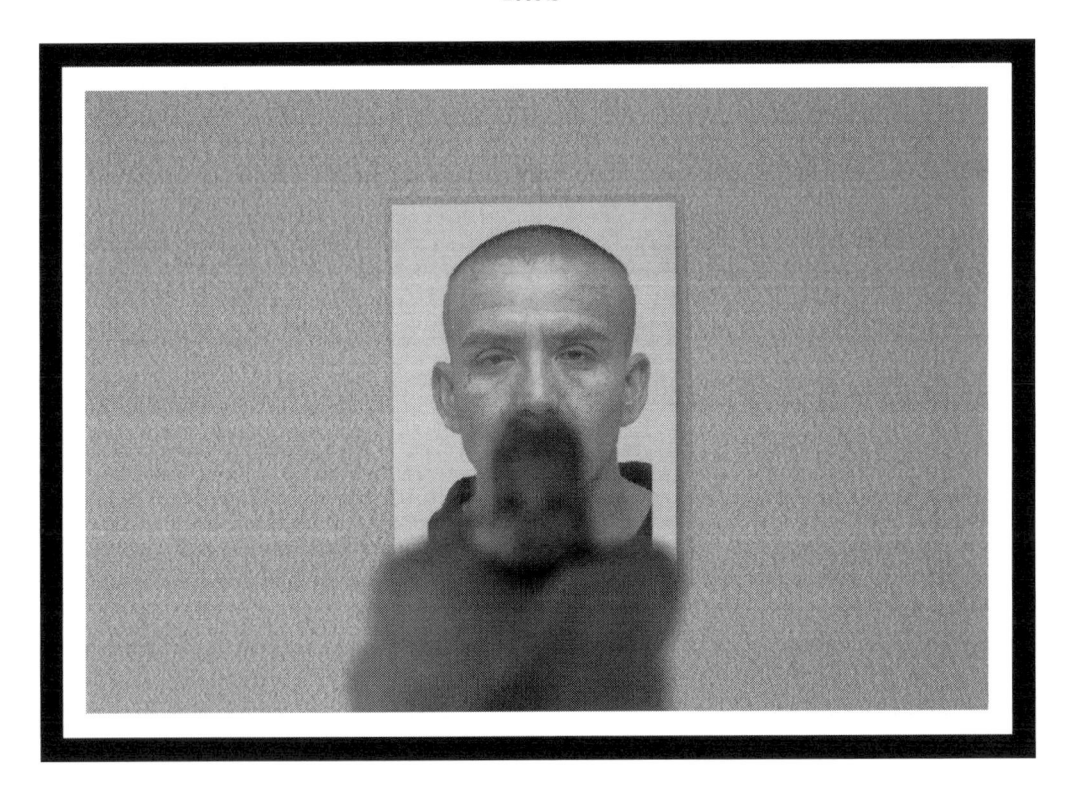

i.2b

NOTE: ZuluFight Sight Picture. Threat is in focus while sights are out of focus.

i.3

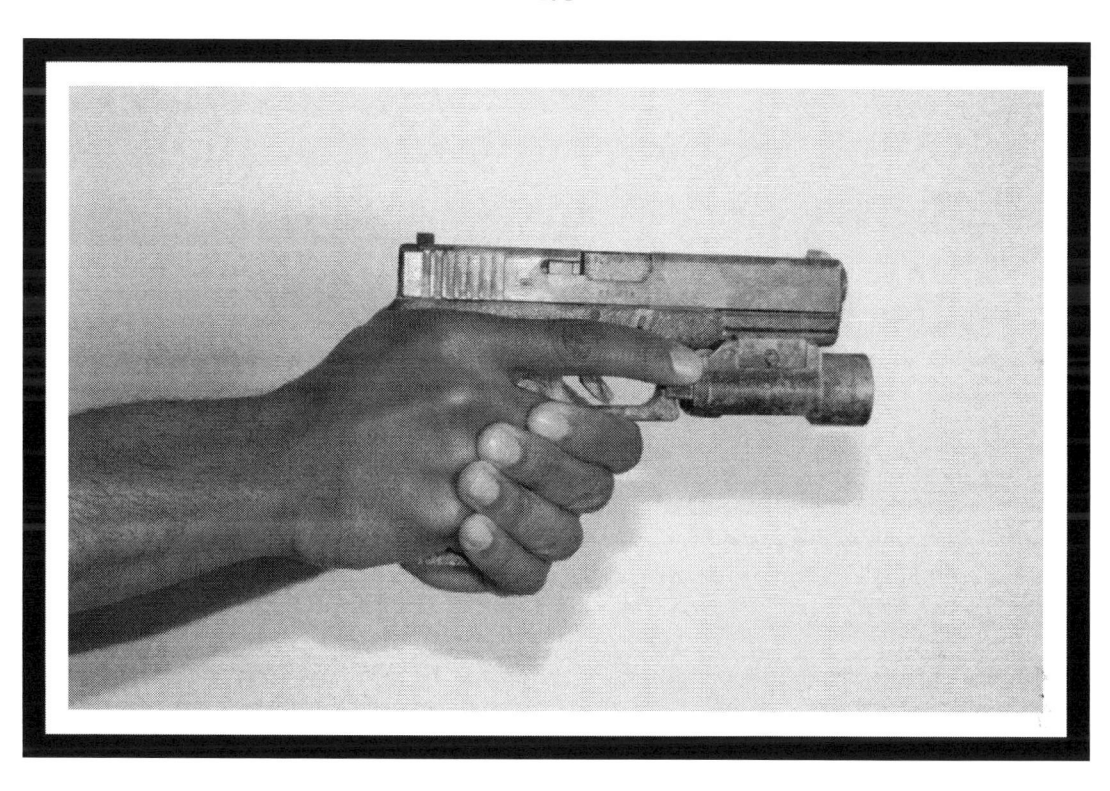

NOTE: Trigger finger rests completely outside trigger guard.

i.4a

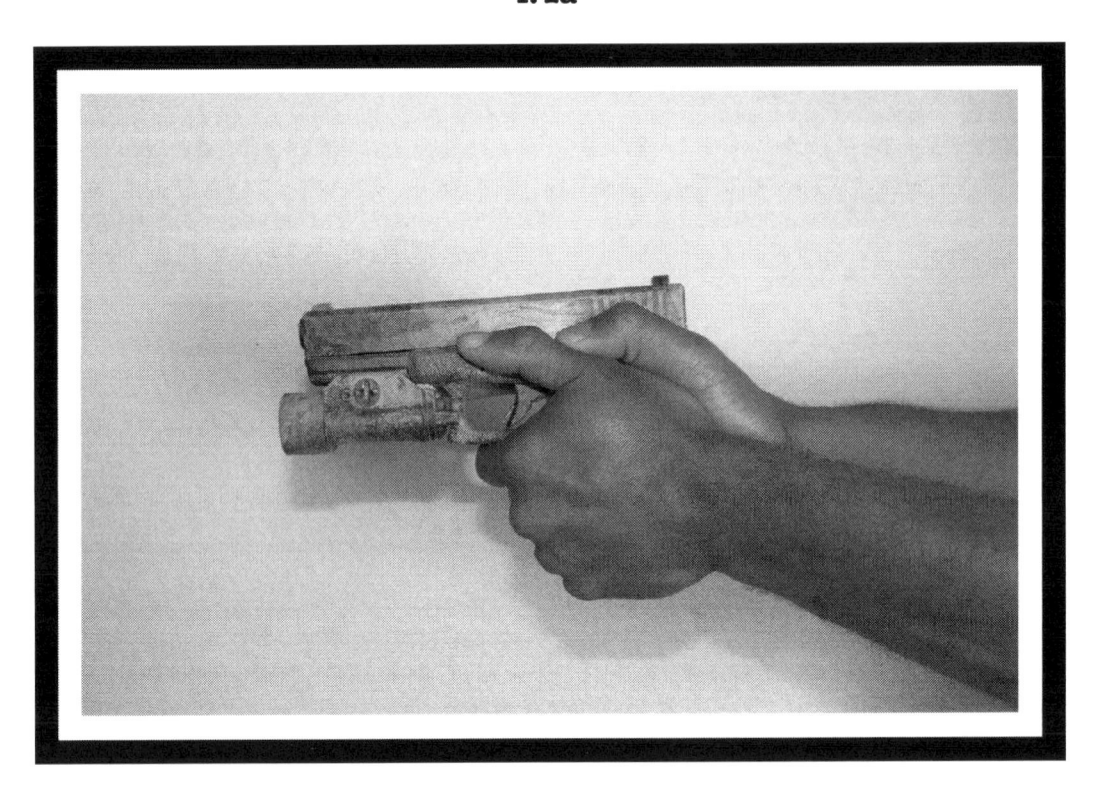

i.4b

NOTE: 70% of grip should come from fingers of support hand.
This allows for consistent & uninhibited trigger squeeze.

i.5

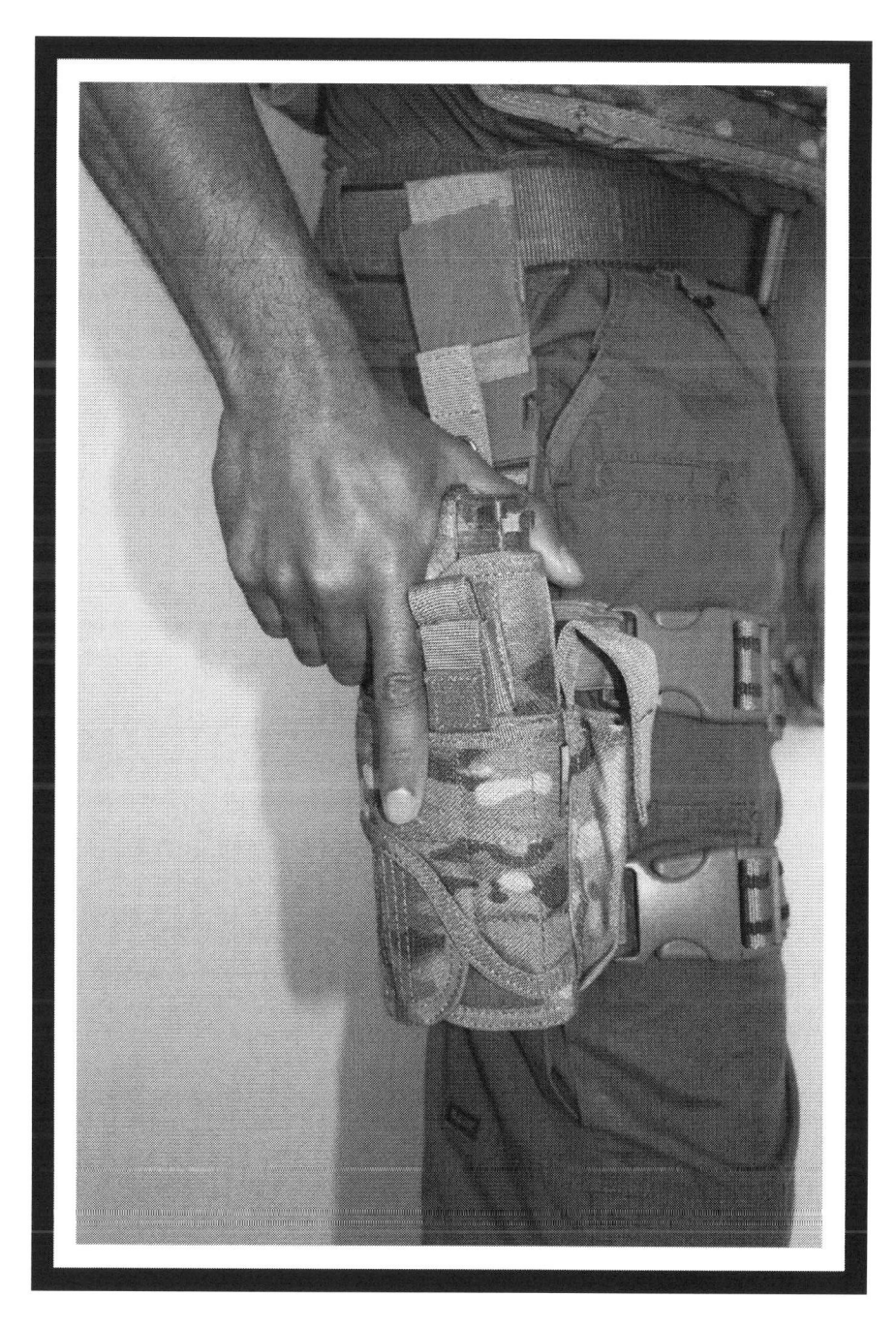

NOTE: Your first grip should be your last. Assure firearm is gripped high in web of thumb & trigger finger is staged outside trigger guard.

i.6

NOTE: Pull firearm straight up avoiding forward movement until muzzle is completely clear. Stage thumb to allow uninhibited placement of support hand.

i.7a

NOTE: Bring sights up and level to eyes not eyes to sights. Feet should be staggered with comfortable bend in knees.

i.7b

NOTE: The Modified Isosceles Stance is hands down the BEST tactical stance. It allows for the best overall mobility. Notice firearms is level with eyes and focus is on threat NOT sights.

i.8

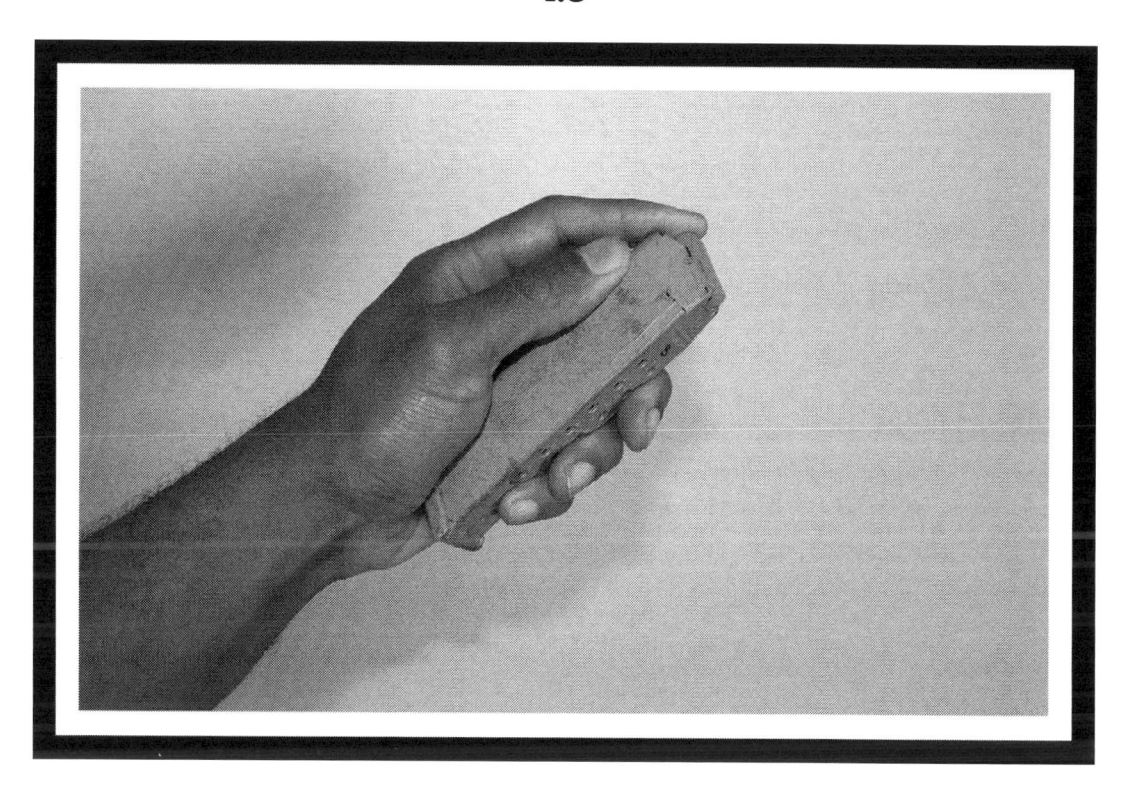

NOTE: Stage index finger on business end of Snap-Cap. This allows for more consistent loading while also assuring Snap-Cap is in correct position.

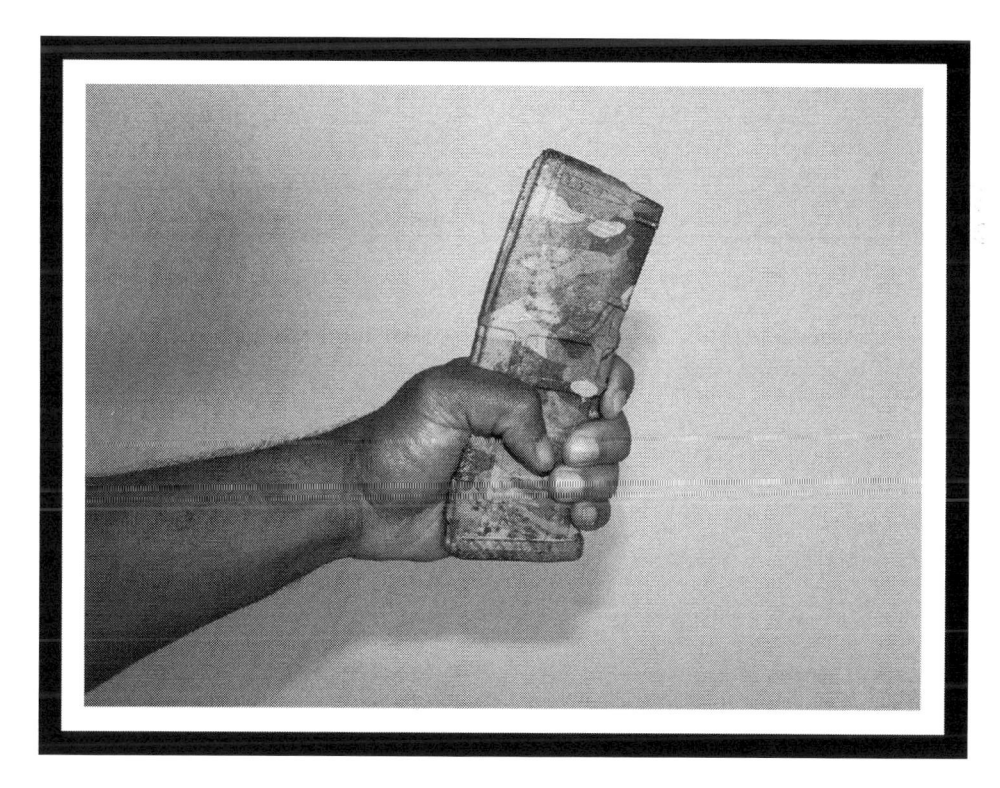

i.9

NOTE: Utilize a fisted grip assuring hand is far to the bottom of the magazine as possible. Make sure business end of magazine is faced away from body.

i.10a

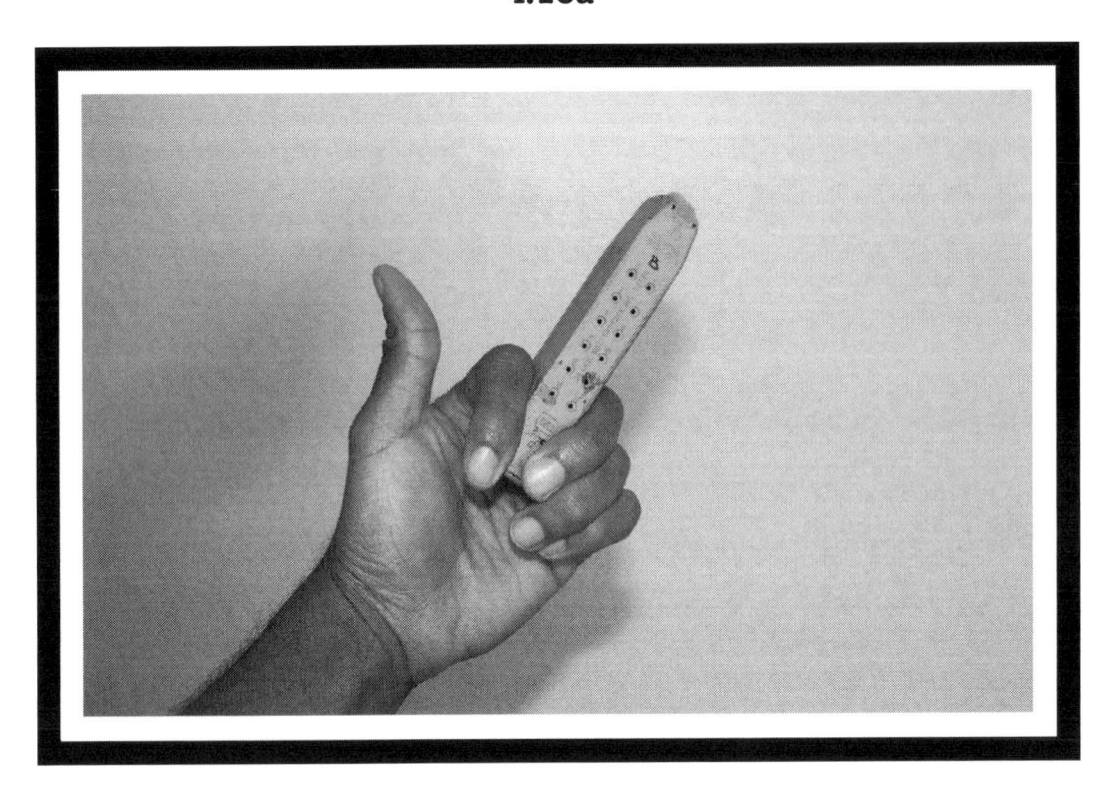

NOTE: Stage magazine so business end is faced away from body. Obtain grip at bottom of magazine placing it between index and middle finger while opening and extending thumb.

i.10b

NOTE: Remove simulated partial magazine from firearm first by placing it in web of thumb. Then insert simulated fresh magazine.

i.11

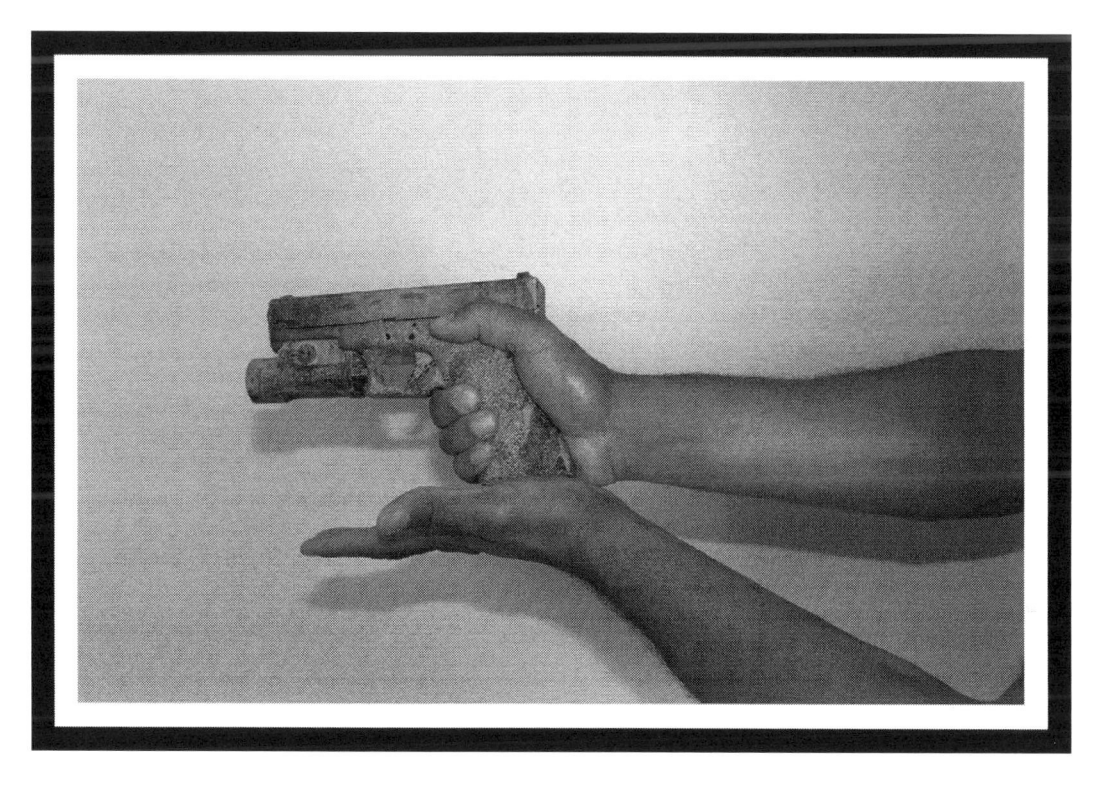

NOTE: Firmly and generously tap the bottom of the magazine to assure it is properly seated.

i.12a

NOTE: Start by slightly canting firearm to allow for visual inspection of ejection port to identify stoppage. Also bring arms back allowing elbows to naturally rest on upper abdomen. This creates a natural working platform to work from allowing you to focus on your Threat while placing firearm in direct focal plane to allow you to still see your firearm utilizing peripheral vision.

i.12b

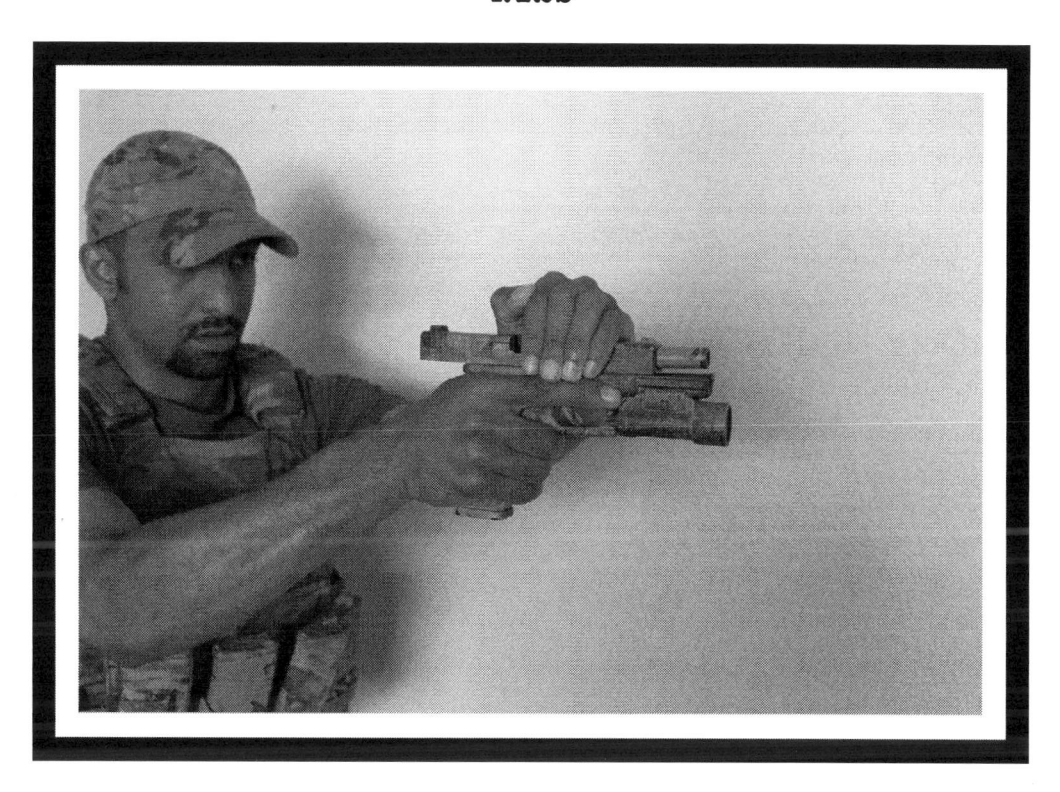

NOTE: Get into the habit of sweeping ejection port while obtaining grip of your slide when attempting to rack. This allows your brain to encode one solid movement for both Type 2 Malfunction clearing and normal racking.

i.12c

NOTE: ALWAYS obtain an over-handed firm grip towards rear of slide. Assure finger is outside trigger guard. Push forward with gun hand while pulling back with support hand to rack slide.

i.12d

NOTE: Release grip of slide after pulling it all the way to the rear. Allow slide to slam forward on its own while also allowing support hand to naturally fling back towards chest. This assures your first round will properly load.

i.13a

i.13b

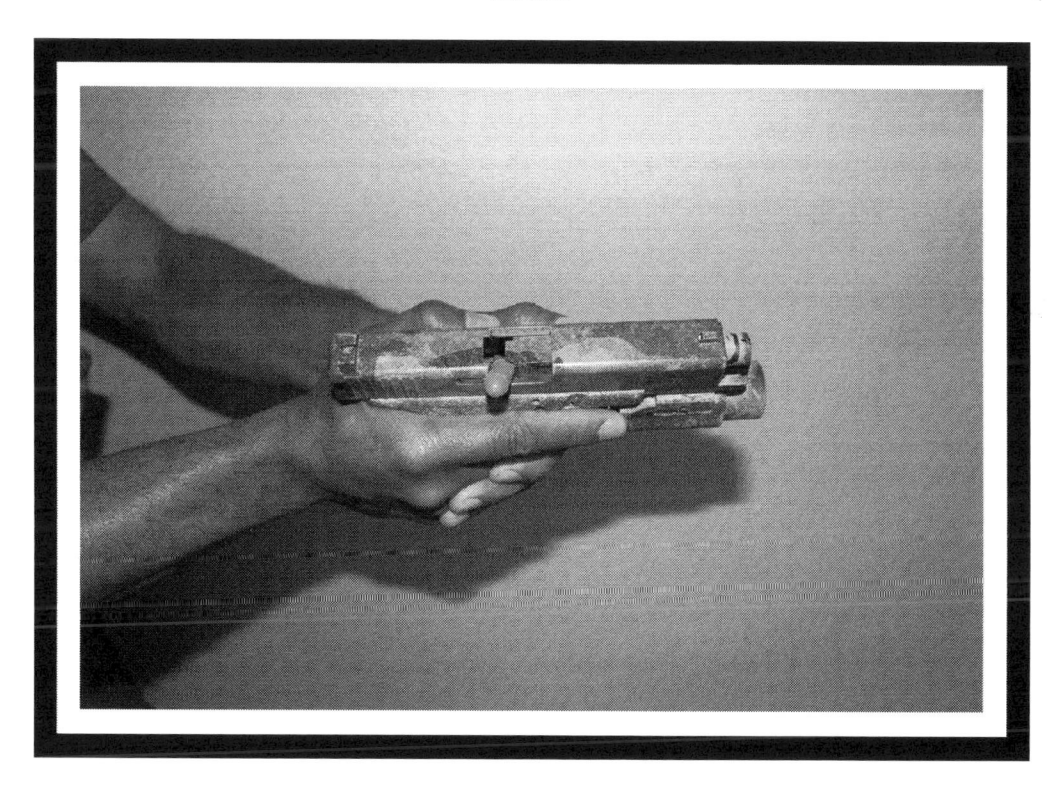

NOTE: Type 2 Malfunctions are easily identified by the spent casing which hangs from the ejection port. This is the most common malfunction in combat situations due to a constantly changing shooting position. Typically occurs due to limp wristing while shooting or an increase in yaw on the firearm as it's in the process of recoil
due to abrupt movement by the shooter.

i.14a

i.14b

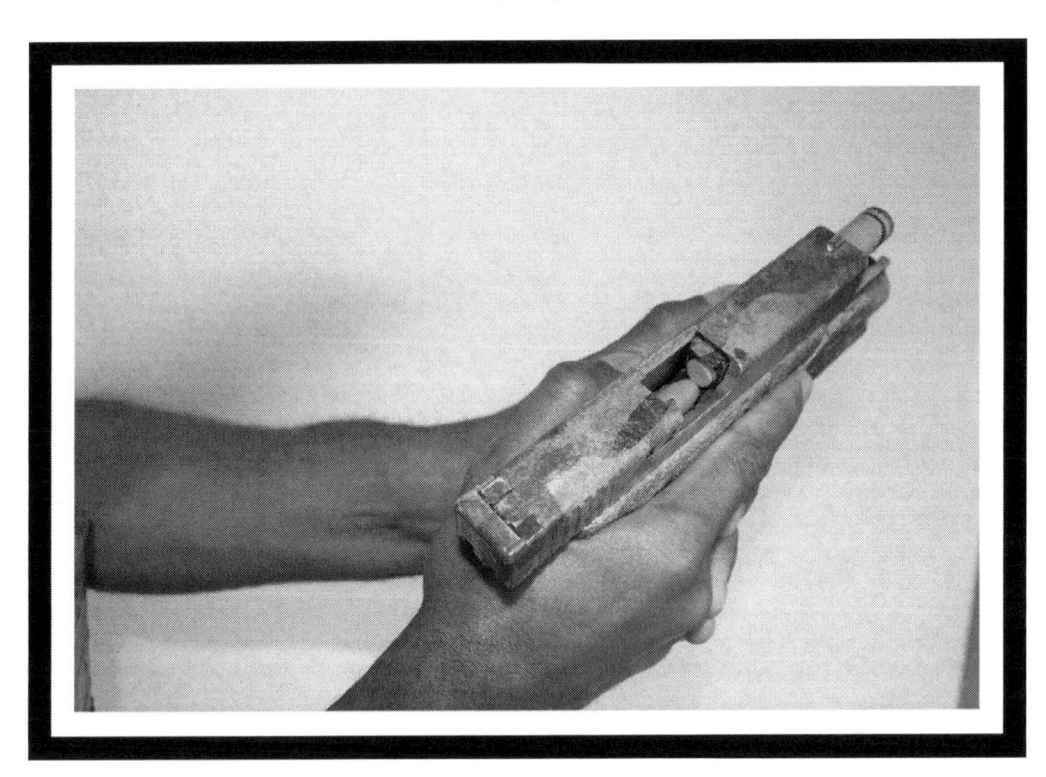

NOTE: Type 3 Malfunctions are almost exclusively caused by a faulty magazine especially handguns. This is a VERY bad malfunction during a gunfight as it will take you out of the fight for a while. For this reason, if you notice this in training, discard, replace and or repair the magazine prior to carrying that magazine for defensive use.

i.15

NOTE: Your cheek weld should not change. Similar to a handgun, bring the sight level to your eyes not your eyes to the sights. Memorize this position and pay attention to the point at which the toe of the butstock rests on your shoulder. This is your "Index" point allowing you to simply pivot the rifle down into Index Ready or up to your shooting position.

i.16

NOTE: Your Tactical Stance is a vital ingredient to your overall fighting solution. The best most practical position should consist of a staggered stance with a comfortable bend in your knees. You should easily be able to move in any direction while also being able to absorb physical contact from any direction. This position should NOT change during the draw or while shooting and is the basis for a Modified Isosceles Stance.

i.17a

NOTE: It's vital that you begin from a completely relaxed stance. Assure that you're not tense. Remember you're training to respond from a position of 'Rest' with both arms dangling at your side.

i.17b

NOTE: It's vital that you begin from a completely relaxed stance. Assure that you're not tense. Remember you're training to respond from a position of 'Rest' while comfortably folding hands in front of you.

i.17c

NOTE: It's vital that you begin from a completely relaxed stance. Assure that you're not tense. Remember you're training to respond from a position of 'Rest' while comfortably folding hands behind your back.

i.17d

NOTE: It's vital that you begin from a completely relaxed stance. Assure that you're not tense. Remember you're training to respond from a position of 'Rest' while comfortably folding hands behind your head.

i.17e

NOTE: Learning to instinctively drop items already in your hands is one of the most vital skills you should acquire. Studies show your natural reaction while under attack is to quickly and tightly close your hands. This posses a major hazard as it sets you up for trying to grab your firearm while still holding onto objects. This is a great way to override your natural response for a Tactical Squared Response.

i.18a

NOTE: The only difference between this shooting position and i.7a & i.7b, is that it's performed while seated. The firearm is still fully extended and brought up to eye level while engaging your Threat.

i.18b

NOTE: This position is slightly different and indented to resemble shooting from a confined space like a car seat, movie theater seat or similar. Your arms are in the same position as C.Q.B. Ready i.19a & i.19b. Your elbows are brought tight against your sides and your firearm placed directly in front of you and level. From this position your torso becomes a turret mounted gun. You aim by simply squaring your shoulders towards your Threat.

i.18c

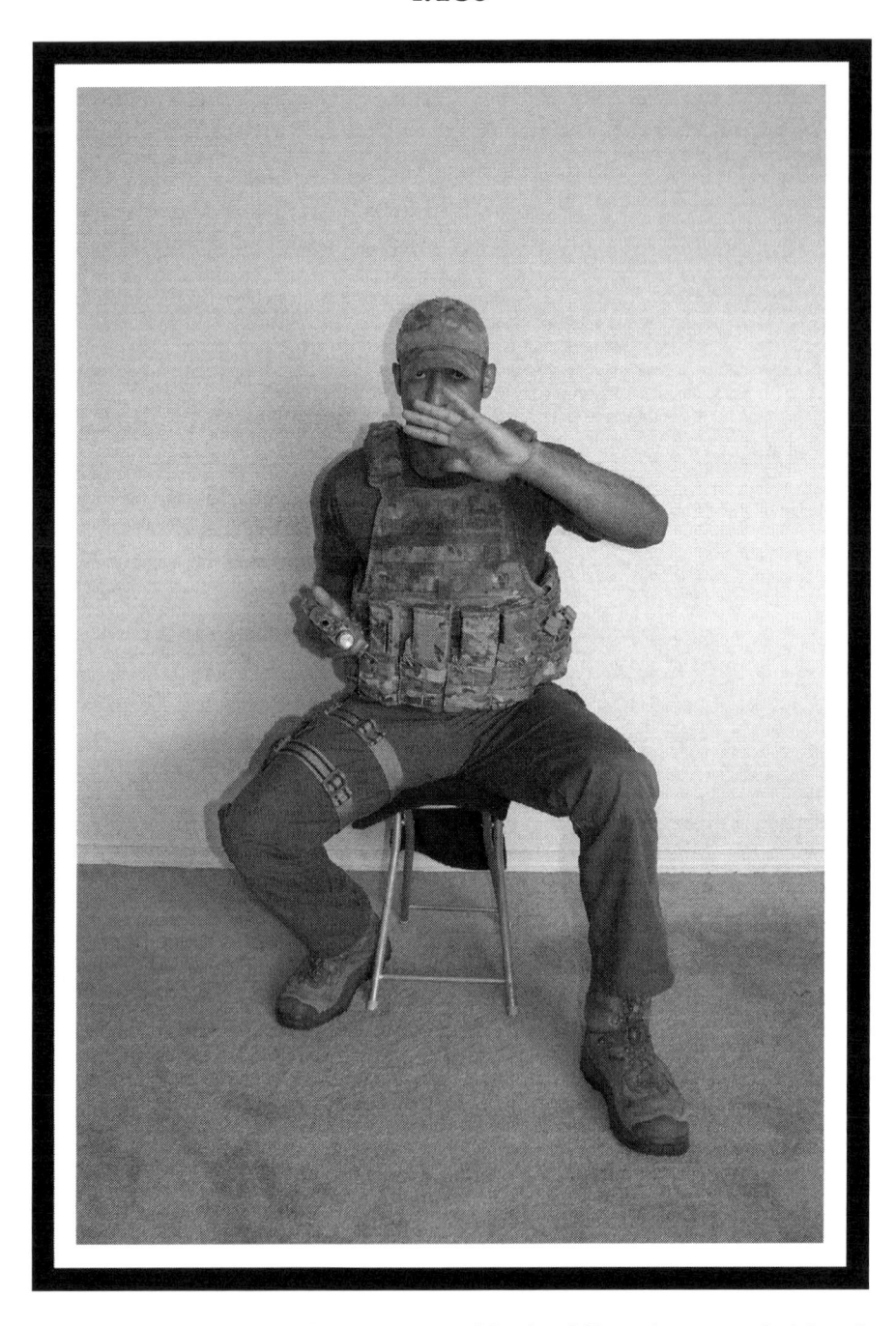

NOTE: This position is the same as Close Ready i.22a & i.22b and is intended for shooting from extremely confined spaces when your Threat is within two feet of you. Simply lock your gun arm into and tight against your side. When shooting from this position, it is vital that you OVERGRIP. Doing so will greatly decrease the chances for a Type 2 Malfunction and encode the strongest one-handed grip possible.

i.19a

NOTE: This position is a perfect shooting platform at close quarters but is also the natural position to obtain a two-handed grip. Your elbows are brought tight against your sides and your firearm placed directly in front of you and level. From this position your torso becomes a turret mounted gun. You aim by simply squaring your shoulders towards your Threat.

i.19b

NOTE: The key to maintaining a level firearm from this position is to lock your wrists and positioning your elbows against your sides as opposed to resting them on your stomach.

i.20a

NOTE: SUL is Portuguese for 'South' the direction of the muzzle. Obtaining this grip is easily performed by indexing both thumbs together remembering the firearm always rests on top of your support hand.

i.20b

NOTE: SUL is the most practical handgun carry position as it provides the safest muzzle disciple while also allowing for ease of draw. SUL is also the safest handgun carry position while moving and or maneuvering around obstacles.

i.20c

NOTE: Drawing from SUL is easy. Simply pivot your thumbs while lifting and pushing your handgun up and out. As you extend your arms, allow your support hand to naturally pivot into your two-handed grip.

i.21a

NOTE: Proper draw from a holster requires attention to detail. Remember it all starts with proper grip i.5. Also remember to stage your support hand at the C.Q.B. Ready position.

i.21b

NOTE: Remember your initial draw-stoke is accomplished by pulling the handgun straight up until it completely clears the holster i.6. Then simply transition your elbow down while pushing your arm forward to meet your support hand at C.Q.B. Ready.

i.22a

NOTE: Close Ready is intended for firing from contact distance or within two feet. Simply lock your gun arm tight against your side with an OVERGRIP of the handgun. Accurate shot placement is similar to C.Q.B. Ready. Utilize your torso and squared shoulders as a sort of turret aiming device.

i.22b

NOTE: It's important to raise your support hand in front of you. It's inevitable that at this distance you will make physical contact with the Threat. Having your support arm positioned in this manner will help provide a solid defensive posture while also giving you the ability to maintain safe distance so your firearm can properly function and reload. Making contact on your Threat with the muzzle while shooting will turn your semi-auto handgun into a single-shot paperweight.

i.23a

NOTE: Reload Ready is accomplished by bringing your gun elbow in tight against your abdomen and side while resting your bicep against your pectoral muscle. This positions your firearm in your direct focal plane while also allow you to maintain visual clarity of your Threat while still seeing your firearm peripherally.

i.23b

NOTE: Reload Ready places your firearm in the most natural position for two-handed manipulation even in complete darkness. This is a position our brains are already instinctively comfortable in and is where your hands naturally meet. Remember to train yourself to manipulate your firearm and reloads while maintaining focus on your Threat NOT the firearm.

i.24a

NOTE: Index Ready is accomplished by simply looking forward naturally while pivoting the toe of the butstock into your Natural Cradle Rest and cheek-weld. DON'T move your head to the weapon, pivot the weapon to your cheek. You shouldn't feel any strain on your neck, just look forward naturally.

i.24b

NOTE: Index Ready affords the shooter the ability of an unobstructed view of the Threat and his surroundings while also affording quick and easy use of his Long Gun.

i.25a

NOTE: Low Index Ready is essentially the SUL Long Gun position. It still utilizes the toe of the butstock as the pivot point. However, to acquire this position, the shooter simply pivots the rifle towards its side while brining his support hand down and in towards his support thigh.

i.25b

NOTE: Low Index Ready is the ideal Long Gun carry position for movement and or maneuvering around obstacles while assuring safe muzzle discipline.

i.26a

NOTE: Check Left. After Action Scan is vital to maintaining effective situational awareness. During direct contact with your Treat, your body will naturally cause your vision to focus on your Threat which such a degree of clarity that everything else around you fades out of view. Encoding proper After Action Scans will allow your brain to literally recalibrate and allow for you to regain normal visual function.

i.26b

NOTE: Now check right. Don't get lazy in training! Remember you're teaching yourself to ACTIVELY look or seek for something. You're not simply moving your head. Scan and SEEK out possible Threats and or positions of possible cover. Remember to look back at your Threat each time you scan from left to right.

i.26c

NOTE: Now it's time to look behind you. Start by looking over your left shoulder. Remember to cognitively identify an object while doing so in training. This trains your brain to instinctively SEEK as opposed to blindly gaze.

i.26d

NOTE: Now it's time to look over your right shoulder. As you transition right, be sure to identify your Threat to assure they're no-longer a threat. As you look over your right shoulder you should also cognitively identify an object behind you. Our ingenious ABCs Tactical Training Aides are the best way to perfect your After Action Scans. They're inexpensive and extremely easy to use. Use them each time you train.

i.27a

NOTE: This is your Rifle Reload Ready Position which starts by observing the ejection port to identify the stoppage prior to reloading or clearing the malfunction. Notice how the weapon is brought towards eye level of the shooter while still allowing the shooter to easily track his Threat. If the stoppage requires a reload, press the mag-release button as you quickly spin your rifle 180°. This allows the magazine to fall with ease due to centrifugal force.

i.27b

NOTE: As you whipped your weapon around so your magazine flies freely, you have also obtained proper grip of a fresh magazine. The is naturally cradled in the crook of the shooting arm with the butstock resting against the lower bicep. This allows for ease of weapon manipulation while also placing the weapon in your direct field of view.

i.27c

NOTE: Insert your simulated fresh magazine, tap it in then tug down on it to assure it's fully seated.

i.27d

NOTE: Now it's time to charge your rifle. It's HIGHLY suggested that you actually teach yourself to PRESS the magazine release button. Many people choose to slap the side of their rifle with the palm of their hands. Doing this is very inefficient. There's a much higher chance of missing the button under stress requiring you to slap the side of your rifle multiple times. Teaching yourself to press the button assures the rifle will charge every time.

i.27e

NOTE: Now it's time to go back to war and KILL your Threat before they kill you. Remember your cheek-weld doesn't change simply because you did a reload. It should be in the same exact place.

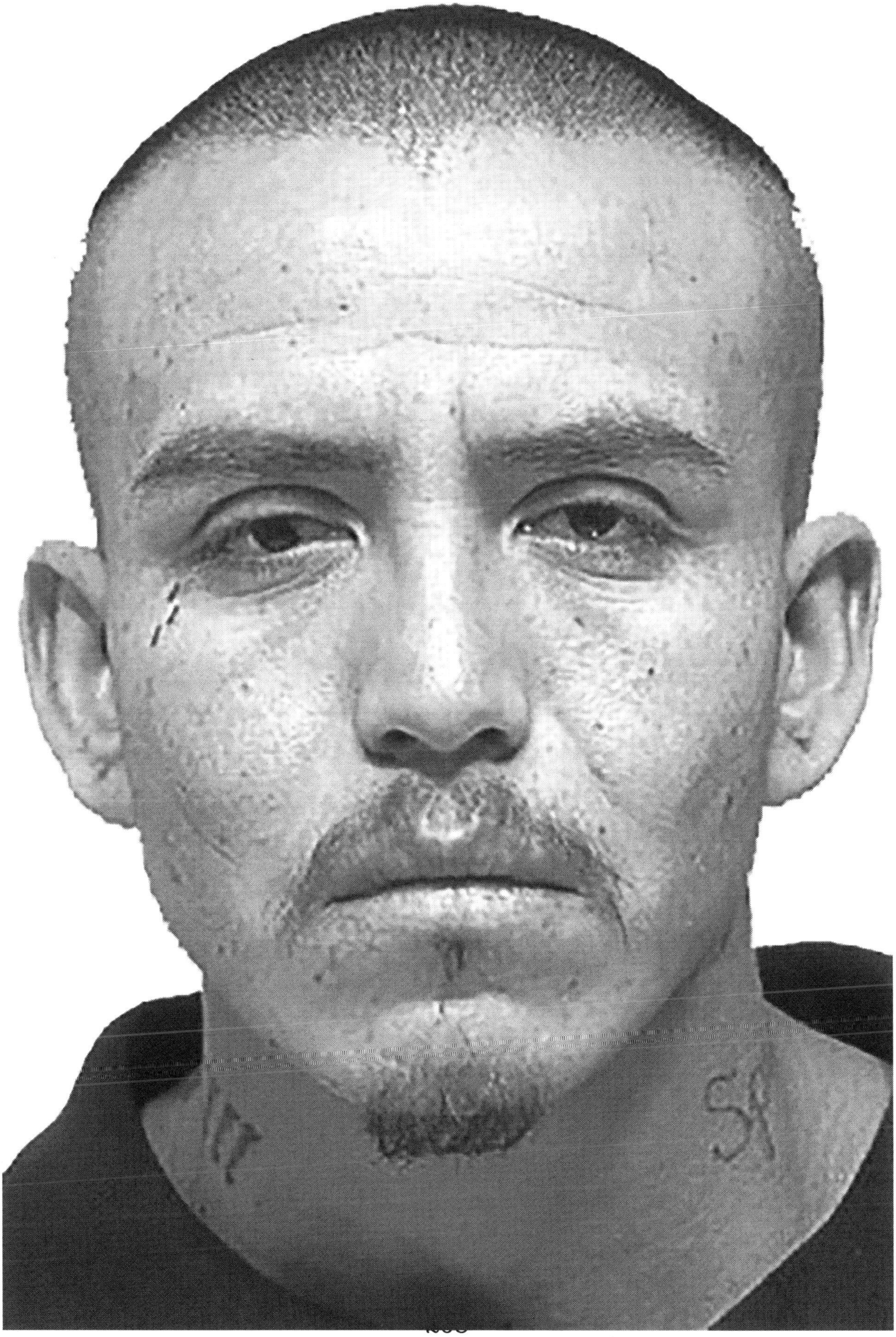

ABCs Tactical Training Aides

- Stay Aware & Stay Alive -

Your ability to maintaining tactically sound situational awareness deadly encounters can mean the difference between winning or losing and losing is something you can't afford. ABCs are the foundation of communication. It's something you learned way back in preschool. ABCs Tactical Training Aides are the ABCs of Tactical Awareness.

Due to a Stress Cocktail of physiological & psychological effects deadly encounters have on our bodies, maintaining 360° awareness greatly diminishes. Training your eyes to 'SEEK' other threats or hazards, areas of cover or concealment, avenues of escape as well as innocent bystanders is critical and ABCs Tactical Training Aides are the best way to achieve the highest levels of Situational Awareness.

Consist sting of an assortment of easily identified, different colored shapes overlaid with Alpha Numerics, ABCs Tactical Training Aides offer a wide range of Tactical Identification choices. These ingenious placard devices can be attached to nearly any surface in almost any training environment on Land or Sea and are the most practical, effective and easy to use tactical training Aides around. Not only are ABCs Tactical Training Aides effective with any type of Dry or Live Fire firearms training, but they're just as beneficial and can greatly enhance many other types of tactical training disciplines.

Take your Tactical Awareness to an unheard of level no matter how stressful or intense the battle. Incorporate ABCs Tactical Training Aides in your training program today. Train Today So You're Ready Tomorrow!

Don't Hesitate. Stay Aware TODAY!

zulutactical.com/abcs

ZuluShield

Firearms Legal Defense

Are you prepared for the all-encompassing legal battle you'll face, when you use Deadly Force to protecting of your life or someone else's? The number one most overlooked aspect of Self-Defense is what comes 'After' the incident. In fact, its as much an afterthought to most people as their last breath.

The sad reality is, you can be completely 'Justified' and cleared of all Criminal Wrongdoing, yet still be found 'Liable' in a Civil Wrongful Death lawsuit? The complicated and completely unavoidable obstacles, which immediately follow every Use of Deadly Force, can easily cost anywhere from hundreds of thousands, to well over a million dollars, all for 'Justifiably' defending yourself? Sadly, most armed professionals aren't even prepared for such an occurrence, let alone the everyday privately armed citizen.

However, it's not all doom and gloom. There are practical steps you can take today, to avoid tomorrow's legal onslaught. This step-by-step guide is your preemptive approach for an impenetrable legal defense. ZuluShield is a must have for anyone who either owns a firearm or for those who may one day be forced to defend themselves with a weapon or even with their hands. Whether you're a private citizen or a seasoned police officer, ZuluShield is your ace up the sleeve.

This system is specifically designed to assist in providing the most solid defense for the most complicated legal battles. It will teach you the vitally important steps you must take directly following such an incident, so you avoiding an unpleasant trip to jail? It will also guide you through the most comprehensive proactive approach to preparing for tomorrow's legal battle today.

Get protected today. Learn the secrets for a bulletproof Firearms Legal Defense. Prepare today so you're ready tomorrow!

Don't Hesitate. Get Protected TODAY!

zulutactical.com/zulushield

ZULUTACTICAL

ZuluFight:

Whether you're in need of a replacement or maybe a gift for a friend or family member, getting another copy couldn't be easier. Use the QR Code to the right or visit our website today!

zulutactical.com/zulufight

ZuluWarrior Training Group:

Are you ready to experience the most repeatable, realistic and reliable firearms training program giving you the most practical solution for tomorrow's deadly encounter? Are you ready to learn realistic tactics so you can play Tactical Chess while your threat plays Checkers? Use the QR Code to the right or visit our website today!

zulutactical.com/training

TeamZulu:

Stay up to date with all things *ZULU*. Connect with us on Facebook. Learn why fans from around the World choose *ZULU*. Use the QR Code to the right or visit our website today!

facebook.com/zulutac

Disclaimer

ABSOLUTELY NO FIREARMS AMMUNITION!!!

Instructor Zulu and ZULU TACTICAL LLC assumes no responsibility or liability whatsoever for the use of this firearms training system. ZuluFight Fight To Win System is a Dry-Fire firearms training system. This means FIREARMS AMMUNITION IS COMPLETELY PROHIBITED while performing this firearms training system. Firearms training is inherently dangerous and has the potential to cause serious physical injury and or death. By using this firearms training system, the user assumes sole responsibility and liability. It is the sole responsibility and liability of the user to assure they safely unload the firearm they intend to use before performing this firearms training system. It is the sole responsibility and liability of the user to double and triple check said firearm to assure said firearm is completely unloaded and free from firearms ammunition. It is the sole responsibility and liability of the user to assure said firearm's magazines are also completely unloaded. It is the sole responsibility and liability of the user to also double and triple check said firearm's magazines to assure said magazines are completely unloaded and free from any and all firearms ammunition. It is the sole responsibility and liability of the user that they have COMPLETELY REMOVED ANY AND ALL FIREARMS AMMUNITION FROM THE INTENDED TRAINING AREA prior to attempting this firearms training system. It is the sole responsibility and liability of the user to maintain the highest level of Firearms Safety through the entirety of this firearms training system.

Absolutely no firearms training system, tactic or technique is guaranteed to win a gunfight or deadly attack. Instructor Zulu and ZULU TACTICAL LLC make no guarantees. ZuluFight Fight To Win System is a training tool, selected at the user's sole risk, responsibility and liability. ZuluFight Fight To Win System is designed to provide a scientifically proven method of learning how to safely and efficiently operate a firearm. This is achieved through the science of Procedural Memory Encoding utilizing Kinesthetic Repetitive Conditioning. This training system is intended to be used for educational and training purposes. Although skills gained from this firearms training system can be effective in surviving an armed attack, it is not the intended to be the user's sole response for real-world gunfights. Instead Instructor Zulu and ZULU TACTICAL LLC encourages users to seek professional firearms training from a certified firearms expert like Instructor Zulu and ZULU TACTICAL LLC, to learn how to incorporate skills acquired during their ZuluFight Fight To Win System training sessions, with actual defensive firearms tactics and techniques.